Fermentation
FOR LIFE

100 Easy Japanese Inspired Recipes
Using Probiotic-Rich Ingredients

MISA ENOMOTO

TUTTLE Publishing

Tokyo | Rutland, Vermont | Singapore

Contents

Chapter 4 Make-Ahead Refrigerated Recipes

Chapter 5 Healthy Sweets and Snacks

About the ingredients, cookware and times used in this cookbook:
• Unless otherwise noted the following are used: the skillet approximately 10 inches (26 cm) in diameter, heatproof bowl 5 inches (13 cm) in diameter, and heatproof plate 9.5 inches (24 cm) in diameter.
• Microwave oven heating times are based on a 600-watt oven. For a 500-watt oven, multiply the cooking time by 1.2; for a 700W-oven adjust the cooking time to .8 times the standard time. For a 1000-watt oven, adjust the time by .35. As always, use your judgment.
• Baking times for ovens and toaster ovens are only a guide. Please check how the food is cooking.
• In this book, amazake made from rice koji (not sake lees) and plain yogurt are used.
• Various fermented foods are used in this book, but out of these amazake, kimchi, black vinegar and rice vinegar, gochujang, sake lees, natto, miso, mirin and yogurt are featured and highlighted.

Why I Wrote This Book

Hey there, fermentation fans, you're in good hands! In addition to being a chef, I'm a fermentation master, devoted to introducing delicious fermented preparations at every meal. From your morning meal to midnight snacks, it's never been easier to harness the probiotic powers of fermented foods.

It's not just lip service: I think I use fermented foods in some way at every meal. There are so many options, not just miso, natto, amazake and yogurt but soy sauce, mirin, vinegar, kimchi, cheese and sake. Given the extent of this list, you probably consume far more fermented foods than you realize.

The recipes in this book are simple and easy; they can all readily be produced in your home kitchen. Beyond being accessible, adaptable and fun to make, they also fulfill one other key criterion: they're simply delicious! You'll find yourself going back to these comfort foods and everyday basics over and over again as you add these preparations and flavors to your regular rotation.

I've included a wide range of recipes for you to try and embrace. Of special note, you'll find a variety of fermented rice dishes, non-dashi-based miso soups, salt koji rice and scrumptious stir fries. Make these fermented dishes part of your daily diet and the benefits will be readily apparent. Healthy eating has never been so delicious—or so easy!

—Misa Enomoto

What Is Fermentation Anyway?

It's a word we're hearing more and more these days—fermentation—often coupled with impassioned descriptions touting the healthful, probiotic benefits of fermented foods. We already know these dishes and processes do the body good. We all know what fermentation is. But given its importance to gut health and inner balance, do we really know enough?

Fermentation harnesses the power of microorganisms to transform foods into nutritional powerhouses. Along the way, flavor is enhanced, the profile refining and taking on layers and nuance. It's all about the power of science, right?

Take miso, for example. Simply mixing together soybeans, koji and salt—the basic ingredients—doesn't necessarily taste good in and of itself. However, when these ingredients ferment, as they refine and change over time, various microorganisms such as koji mold, lactic acid bacteria and yeast bacteria join forces to produce both the sweetness and umami that are the hallmarks of a truly superior and highly nutritious miso.

Or let's look at another superfood example featured in this book: natto. Some are unable to embrace this soybean concoction because of its prominent and pungent smell. But those who have discovered its merits celebrate the benefits this potent bundle of concentrated nutrition delivers.

Beneath the surface, too tiny for the eye to see, microorganisms are working their transformative magic, lending your favorite kitchen basics and go-to staples fermented flair. It's a fascinating and healthful daily journey. Are you ready to begin?

Chapter 1

Everyday Recipes

If you're going to do something every day, it helps if it's easy, right? What about this simple formula? Just add miso and a few simple ingredients to a bowl, pour in some hot water, give it a stir and you're good to go. Now this is a kind of simple habit that's good for us! Here, I've gathered a range of everyday preparations you can whip up without any fuss, proving how easy it is to integrate fermented foods into your daily routine.

Miso-Based Fermentation Recipes

Miso comes in a variety of guises, but what is it exactly?

A fermented soybean paste, miso has been a mainstay of the Japanese diet for over 1,300 years. A great source of essential nutrients (including vitamins B12, B2, E and K and dietary fiber) and probiotics that support healthy digestion and slow the effects of aging. It strengthens the immune systems, helps alkalize the body and have been shown to reduce the risks of breast cancer.

Made with soybeans, salt and the fungus (or mold actualy, Aspergillus oryzae) known as koji, miso is typically classified by its koji content and ingredients as well as by its color. The three basic types are identified by the type of grain malt used to produce it: rice malt miso (the most common and popular type), barley malt (or "country-style") and soybean malt miso (or hatcho, known for its deep brown color and intense flavor).

Miso moods: what's your favorite color?

Generally, rice malt miso is made with very simple ingredients: soybeans, rice koji and salt. All you have to do is mix softened soybeans (boiled or steamed), koji mold and salt.

Miso can also be classified by its color, typically coming in three classic "shades." The color is the result of several factors such as the ratio of the ingredients and the amount of time it spends fermenting. The amino acids in the miso react with the sugar and change color. The longer the fermentation process, the darker the color. Awase miso is light brownish yellow, the most common and popular form. With its balanced flavors, it's a go-to option that goes well with a wide range of dishes.

Shiro miso is whitish to light yellow and is sweeter because it isn't fermented as long. Prized for its light flavor, it's a common additive to soups and dressings and is used as a pickle seasoning. Finally, there's the salty-savory punch of aka miso, reddish brown in color and often used with seafood and simmered dishes.

My #1 Tip: Easy-to-Mix Miso

For me, miso is truly an essence, a building block that I use every day. In my home, I keep three different kinds of this wonder substance in one container.

I often combine the three main types of miso, awase, shiro and aka, to create a rainbow of flavors. Or I'll fuse two different flavors of light miso, homemade miso or even sake lees (*sakekasu*). Because these hybrid combinations only serve to enhance the flavor of whatever we're making, we often combine different types to create many of our favorite recipes.

If you keep different types of miso on hand, store them in a single container. Like a painter's palette, you can mix and blend, choosing whatever combination of flavors will exactly complement what you're preparing. Be aware that mold can grow on low-salt versions. After dipping into your miso container, smooth the surface and be sure the container is tightly sealed to prevent it from being exposed to air, oxidizing and drying out.

Here, I've incorporated miso not only into soups but all sorts of dishes—stir fries, dressings and rice dishes. Who knows what uses you'll find for its savory flavors!

Miso Works Well with All Kinds of Dishes

Use miso as a flavor booster in Western-style dishes

Ever-flexible, miso is featured in a range of Japanese-style grilled meats, fish, vegetables, stews and the ubiquitous miso soup that has been embraced worldwide. It's incredibly versatile, so it comes as no surprise that this powerful paste is a great addition to Western cuisine as well.

Take a bolognese or a pasta-style meat sauce, for example. Adding miso gives it a richer and deeper flavor. It's also great in beef stew or with chicken stewed in tomato sauce or coated in a demiglace. I recommend using light brown miso or red miso for these dishes.

Miso makes a wonderful addition to cream-based dishes as well. It can be used in alfredos, gratins, carbonara and other dishes. White miso is also great to have on hand and one of the most common types avaialable in the West. It's probably the one you've been using all along. Why not add the other "colors" of the miso rainbow to your repertoire? Give them all a try!

Adding miso elevates your recipes

Miso is recommended not only for Western-style recipes but really for any kind of dish you're preparing. Adding miso to gyoza dumplings provides an extra punch, while adding it to curry brings a new depth of flavor. I often introduce as a finishing touch to keema curry, which tends to be a bit light in flavor on its own.

If you add just a little bit of miso, you needn't worry about the resulting dish being dominated by the flavor. A little goes a long way! You'll hardly notice that there's miso in there, but the overall dish will certainly take on more depth and complexity. This is the power of miso, truly a behind-the-scenes player offering the simple support and fermented goodness you need.

What Is Mirin?

Mirin imparts a rich and elegant flavor to sauces, soups and broths. It's a subtle fermented seasoning, a type of rice wine similar to sake but with lower alcohol and a higher sugar content. Any number of dishes can be enhanced by using mirin instead of sugar, so give this simple substitute a try.

Organic Sanshu Mirin

A mirin made by Bunjiro Sumiya Shoten in Hekinan City, Aichi Prefecture, Japan. It gives a deep taste. I use it when I want to give my dishes a strong flavor. When black soybeans are stewed with this mirin, it gives them a mellow taste. It is also used as a substitute for liqueur in desserts.

Bunjiro Sumiya Shoten
https://mikawamirin.jp

Ultimate White Mirin

This mirin is from Baba Honten Sake Brewery in Katori City, Chiba Prefecture. It has a gentle sweetness that is delicious even when drunk on its own. It is used for finishing dishes or when you want to add a refined taste. It can also be used as a substitute for syrup in dishes such as almond tofu.

Baba Honten Sake Brewery
https://babahonten.com/

Is mirin a beverage or a seasoning?

It's time mirin is given more of a starring role in your dishes.

The term describes a variety of products, including hon (real) mirin and mirin-style seasoning. The latter version isn't a fermented food but a seasoning made with sugar syrup and other ingredients to bump up the sweetness. Hon mirin contains alcohol, but mirin-style seasoning doesn't. So be sure to pick up the version that's labeled hon mirin.

Hon, for short, be used in a wide range of dishes. Add it to simmered dishes but also turn to it as a sweetener in place of sugar when making stir fries and sauces. It can also be used as a substitute for liqueur when making tiramisu or boiled down to a syrup for almond tofu or other dessert-style delicacies.

And why not sip a glass of delicious hon mirin as a aperitif or digestif? As a potent potable, it's warming and soothing, if not unusually elegant!

I hope that you'll add at least one bottle of mirin to your shelf of staples. You'll be surprised at how often you use it!

"Pour & Eat" Miso Soups

Miso soup is a forgiving and flexible canvas on which you can easily build layers of flavor. It's simplicity is its hallmark. But there are days when you're not up for even this most basic of preparations. You don't want to linger over a hot stove or take the time to whip up a complex dashi stock.

It's exactly for these reasons that "pour and eat" miso exists, for the overworked, the time-pressed or the simply ravenous. It's an easy way to make miso soup by adding your favorite type of miso to a bowl or cup and pouring boiling water over it.

Many purists believe that miso soup must be made with dashi stock. I used to think so too. But one day at a miso shop, they served me a soup highlighting just the taste of the miso on its own. It was made by simply dissolving miso in hot water. And you guessed it: it was so delicious, a revelation!

Since then, pour-and-eat miso has been essential on those busy days when my family is on the go. You can add your favorite dried foods or simple ingredients that don't need to be cooked. The umami flavors and savory tastes will announce themselves right away! Try it and you'll see!

Add hot water. . .

Mix and it's done!

Green Onion and Fried Tofu Skin Miso Soup

You can find the fried tofu skin at an Asian grocery or specialty shop.

Serves 4

Divide 4 tablespoons of miso, a piece of abura-age (fried tofu skin) cut into ⅓-inch (1-cm) strips and minced green onion, to taste, between four bowls. Add just less than 1 cup (235 ml) of boiling water to each and mix well.

Miso

Sakura Shrimp & Dried Daikon Miso Soup

The sakura shrimp adds a luxurious burst of umami.

Serves 4

Divide 4 tablespoons miso, 2 tablespoons kiriboshi daikon (dried daikon radish strips) and 2 tablespoons dried sakura shrimp (tiny dried shrimp) between four bowls. Add just less than 1 cup (235 ml) of boiling water to each and mix well.

Miso

Miso

The nori and fish form the perfect combination.

Nori and Jako Miso Soup

(Serves 4) Add 1 tablespoon of miso and just less than 1 cup (235 ml) of boiling water to each bowl. Mix well. Shred a sheet of nori seaweed and distribute it evenly between the bowls. Add ½ tablespoon of jako (semi-dried whitefish) to each of the bowls.

Miso

This version really accentuates the sweetness of the tomato.

Tomato and Katsuobushi Miso Soup

(Serves 4) Divide 4 tablespoons of miso, 6 quartered cherry tomatoes and 4 pinches of katsuobushi (bonito flakes), to taste, between four bowls. Add just less than 1 cup (235 ml) of boiling water to each and mix well.

Miso

The creamy texture of tororo kombu meets crunchy myoga ginger.

Kombu and Myoga Ginger Bud Miso Soup

(Serves 4) Divide 4 tablespoons of miso and a handful of tororo kombu (thinly shaved kombu) between the bowls. Add just less than 1 cup (200 ml) of boiling water to each and mix well. Slice two myoga ginger buds thinly and divide the pieces between the bowls.

Miso
Gochujang

The spicy flavor wakes up the tongue!

Spicy Miso Soup with Okra and Rice Crackers

(Serves 4) Divide 4 tablespoons miso, 1 teaspoon gochujang and 2 okra pods sliced into rounds between the bowls. Add just less than 1 cup (235 ml) of boiling water to each and mix well. Crush spicy rice crackers (kaki no tane) and divide 2 tablespoons of the pieces between the bowls.

Miso

When you're in the mood to be refreshed.

Umeboshi and Wakame Miso Soup

(Serves 4) Divide 4 tablespoons miso, 4 tablespoons dried cut wakame and 4 umeboshi (torn into small pieces) equally between the bowls. Add 1 cup (235 ml) of boiling water to each and mix well.

Miso

The power of ginger warms the body from the inside out.

Wheat Gluten and Ginger Miso Soup

(Serves 4) Divide 4 tablespoons of miso, 4 teaspoons of temari-fu (dried ball-shaped wheat gluten) and 2 teaspoons of grated ginger in equal portions between the bowls. Add 1 cup (235 ml) of boiling water to each and mix well.

Miso

A miso soup that's a hit with kids!

Corn and Cheese Miso Curry Soup

(Serves 4) Divide 4 tablespoons miso, 2 tablespoons canned whole corn kernels and 2 teaspoons curry powder equally between two bowls. Add 1 cup (235 ml) of boiling water to each bowl. Divide 2 tablespoons of pizza cheese equally between the bowls.

Miso

Western-flavored miso works well too!

Broccoli Sprout and Bacon Miso Soup

(Serves 4) Divide 4 tablespoons miso paste and a slice of cooked bacon (cut into ⅓-inch/ 1-cm pieces) between the bowls. Add 1 cup (235 ml) boiling water to each bowl and stir well. Divide 1 cup sprouts equally between the bowls and drizzle with olive oil to taste.

Double Fermented Soups

Fermented foods are great on their own but often taste even better when combined. Miso soup, in particular, can take on plenty of layers of fabulous fermented flavor. Enhance the power of fermentation and warm up your body from the inside at the same time by having your dishes do double duty.

Miso

Kimchi

Kimchi and Mountain Yam Miso Soup

The mountain yam adds texture to this simple soup whose spicy flavor is addictive.

Serves 2

½ cup (100 g) mountain yam or yuca
1⅔ cups (400 ml) dashi stock
1 cup (100 g) napa cabbage kimchi
4 teaspoons miso
Diagonally thinly sliced green onion, to garnish

1 Peel the mountain yam or yuca, place in a plastic bag and break into bite-sized pieces by bashing with a rolling pin.
2 Heat the dashi stock in a saucepan over medium heat, bring to a boil, add the mountain yam and cook for 1–2 minutes. Reduce the heat, add the kimchi and dissolve 4 teaspoons of miso. Arrange in two serving bowls and sprinkle with the green onion.

Salmon and Sake Lees Vegetable Miso Soup

A healthy and hearty miso soup proves the perfect vehicle for the subtleties of salmon.

Serves 2

1 cup (100 g) napa cabbage leaves
½ carrot (about 1.7 oz/50 g)
2 green onions
¼ lb (about 100 g) salmon fillet
Salt, to taste
2 cups (500 ml) dashi stock
2 tablespoons sake lees
A 1-inch (2.5-cm) piece ginger, cut into thin strips
3 tablespoons white miso (or 2 tablespoons light miso)
Sliced yuzu or lemon peel, to taste

1 Cut the napa cabbage into bite-sized pieces. Peel the carrot, cut in half lengthwise and cut into ¼-inch (3 mm) half-moon slices. Cut the green onions into thin diagonal slices. Cut the salmon into quarters and sprinkle with a pinch of salt.

2 Heat the dashi stock and sake lees in a saucepan over medium heat, add the napa cabbage, carrot and green onion (**photo a**), then cover and simmer for 4–5 minutes. Add the salmon and ginger, cover and simmer for 3 minutes more.

3 Reduce the heat, stir in the miso until dissolved and serve topped with julienned yuzu or lemon peel.

Note

There are two types of sake lees: kneaded lees, which are cream-like, and lees that come in sheet form. If you're using sheet lees, place 1½ tablespoons in a small heatproof container, add 1 tablespoon of water, then cover loosely with cling wrap and microwave for 40 seconds. Mix well before using.

Miso

Sake Lees

All About Amazake

What kind of fermented food is amazake?

There are many different amazake products on the market, and if you're an amazake addict like me, it's fun to try them all. On the other hand, I also make my own all the time. Amazake is, after all, simple and easy. All you need is rice koji and hot water! You can also use rice or congee, but I prefer to keep it simple. So I make it using rice koji.

Sweet yet without any sugar added to it, it's an enigmatic superfood. Let me briefly explain the principle. The sweetness is produced by an enzyme in the rice koji, amylase, that converts the starch in the rice koji into glucose and other sugars. This is what makes the rice taste sweet. When you chew a mouthful of rice for a while, you can detect the slight hint of sweetness, right? That is because amylase in human saliva converts the rice starches into sugar. The amazake process simply helps that process along, elevating the sweet profile I've come to crave.

Homemade amazake is so easy to make!

The homemade amazake introduced here is made by simply pouring hot water into a thermal jar and then adding rice koji to it. It's just that easy!

Be careful about the temperature though. It's important to keep a consistent temperature of about 140°F (60°C) to be sure the rice koji enzymes do their work.

If the temperature is too low or too high, your amazake won't acquire the proper sweetness. Bring the rice koji to room temperature, measure the temperature of the hot water carefully, then mix it quickly and put on the lid. The resulting amazake will have a gentle, delicous sweetness. You'll find yourself coming back to it again and again, a healthy addiction! If you're not going to drink or cook with it right away, it can always be frozen in plastic bags.

Just Add Hot Water! How to Make Easy Amazake

Making your own amazake is easy once you get the hang of it, so give it a try and take yet another step on your fermentation journey. Marinate meat or seafood in it to activate the amazing enzymes and unlock their transformative power!

Makes 1⅔ cups (400 ml)

STORAGE TIME: This keeps in the refrigerator for one week, and in a freezer bag in the freezer for a month.

1 cup (200 g) dried rice koji (at room temperature)
1¼ cups (300 ml) hot water

1 Put just less than a cup (220 ml) of boiling water and ⅓ cup (80 ml) cold water (or 1¼ cups/300 ml 160°F/70°C lukewarm water) in a thermal soup jar and cool to 149°F/65°C (**photo a**).
2 Add the rice koji and mix quickly (**photo b**). Close the lid of the jar securely and leave it at room temperature for 8 hours.
3 Taste, and if it's the right degree of sweetness, blend it until it's smooth (**photo c**). Transfer it to a clean storage container, then store it in the refrigerator.

Note
It's important not to let the temperature drop too much, so mix it quickly then seal the jar with the lid. As with commercially made undiluted amazake, this homemade amazake will have the right thickness for drinking as is. I recommend drinking it chilled in the summer and warming it up in a small pan in the winter.

Two Types of Amazake

What's the difference between them?

Amazake is readily available in Asian grocery stores, online and at some health food stores. But did you know that there are two types of amazake made from different ingredients often mistaken for the same thing? One type is made with rice koji, and the other is amazake made with sake lees and sugar.

Rice koji amazake is made with rice koji and hot water (sometimes steamed rice or rice porridge are also used). It uses the power of enzymes derived from rice koji to convert the starch in the rice koji into sugar, which naturally gives it a sweet taste. On the other hand, amazake made from sake lees is made by diluting sake lees with hot water and adding sugar to sweeten it. The main type sold these days is rice koji amazake, which is the type used in this book. I also like sake lees amazake because it's rich in nutrients and, just as important, delicious. But rice koji amazake doesn't use sugar and does not contain alcohol, making it safe for anyone to drink, including children and pregnant women. Sake lees are the dregs left from making sake, so there's still a trace amount of alcohol in them. Although most of the alcohol is removed in the process of making amazake, a little remains, so caution is required for those sensitive to or avoiding alcohol.

Try different varieties until you find the ones you like best!

Nowadays, there are so many varieties of amazake made from rice koji available. Well-stocked Asian grocery and natural-food stores have a range of options, and you can even find regional brands online.

Different types of koji, such as brown rice, black rice and white rice koji, are used. In addition, amazake from a sake brewery and one from a miso maker may taste different because of the different characteristics of the koji used.

Try a variety of amazakes and experiment to find your favorites.

Amazing Amazake!

Amazake has been attracting attention for its taste and health benefits. In my home, it's used as a sugar substitute in a range of our favorite dishes, and of course we love to drink it as is. Let's take a closer look at these two types of taste treats.

An amazake with a refreshing sour flavor

Amazake made by the Niida brewery in Koriyama City, Fukushima Prefecture. This amazake is made from white malted rice, which is rare, and is characterized by its refreshing sourness and that it is easy to drink. It is also suitable for those who dislike the strong sweetness of amazake. I recommend drinking it as it is without using it for cooking.

Niida Honke
https://1711.jp/

An amazake made with rice koji only

Amazake made by Hakkai Brewery in Minamiuonuma City, Niigata Prefecture. Using sake-making techniques, the company makes rice koji from highly polished rice to bring out a gentle sweetness without the use of sugar. It is delicious with a strong sweet taste. This brand is easily available at supermarket around Japan.

Hakkai Brewery
https://www.amasake.co.jp

Fermented Drinks and Beverages

In my family, we drink black vinegar mixed with amazake every day. It's a quick and easy blend that's packed with nutrients and a convenient way to add even more fermented foods to your daily intake!

I recommend drinking amazake-based drinks for breakfast. With so many options, it's easy to make them part of your daily ritual and routine. Amazake is full of glucose, which activates the brain and gets you going in the morning.

Black vinegar and vinegar-based drinks are refreshing and are a great caffeine-free way to take an afternoon break.

Here I've come up with a variety of easy-to-make fermented drinks, some with fruit, others using tea, and ones that can be served cold or hot. I'm sure you'll find a new favorite to embrace and, as always, adapt these recipes to taste to make them your own!

Cold Amazake Drinks

Amazake is a nutrition powerhouse, a superfood whose time has come (see page 22). Containing high levels of B vitamins, which are effective in relieving fatigue, and glucose, which provides an immediate energy boost, amazake is ideal for summer when our active bodies need a bit of extra fuel. Just mix amazake with a spoon or in a blender for a quick and easy drink, and feel the power of this powerful fermented food flooding through you.

Ingredients and Directions - All 1 serving

Amazake Green Tea

Amazake Coffee Jelly Drink

Amazake Lassi

Amazake Tomato Juice

Amazake Strawberry Soy Milk

Amazake Pineapple Soda

Directions on page 26

Amazake Green Tea

You'll love the rich, creamy flavor!

In a glass, mix ½ cup (100 ml) of brewed hojicha and ½ cup (100 ml) of amazake (undiluted type) with a spoon.

Amazake

Amazake Tomato Juice

Tomato juice makes it thick and rich.

In a glass, mix ⅖ cup (100 ml) of no-salt-added tomato juice and ½ cup (100 ml) of amazake (undiluted type) with a spoon. Top with basil leaves if desired, and drizzle with olive oil.

Amazake

Amazake Coffee Jelly Drink

A grown-up accent taps the bitterness of coffee.

Put 2½ oz (70 g) of coffee jelly in a glass and mash gently with a spoon. Add ½ cup (100 ml) of amazake (undiluted type) and mix with a spoon.

Amazake

Amazake Lassi

A double fermented drink that contains both amazake and yogurt.

In a blender, combine ⅔ cup (150 ml) of undiluted amazake, ¼ cup (50 ml) of plain yogurt and 1 teaspoon of lemon juice. Pour into a glass and garnish with mint, if desired.

Amazake   Yogurt

Amazake Strawberry Soy Milk

The tart strawberries pair perfectly with the sweetness of the amazake.

Put 4 prepared strawberries in a glass, and mash them with a fork. Add ½ cup (100 ml) of amazake (undiluted type) and ¼ cup (50 ml) of soy milk (unsweetened) and mix gently.

Amazake

Amazake Pineapple Soda

A refreshing flavor ideal for summer.

In a glass, mix ¼ cup (50 ml) pineapple juice and ½ cup (100 ml) amazake (undiluted type) with a spoon. Add ½ cup (100 ml) of soda water and top with cubed pineapple, if desired.

Amazake

* I use rice-koji-based non-alcoholic amazake for these recipes.

Hot Amazake Drinks

On days when you're feeling a chill, a warm amazake works wonders. Amazake promotes intestinal health, relieves constipation and improves immunity to colds and other illnesses. But once you feel its warming powers, you won't be thinking of anything else.

Black Sesame and Soy Milk Amazake with Kinako

A gentle Japanese taste with the richness of black sesame and kinako, or roasted soybean powder.

In a small saucepan, heat ½ cup (100 ml) of amazake (undiluted type) and ½ cup (100 ml) of unsweetened soy milk over medium heat. Add 1 teaspoon each of black sesame seeds and kinako.

Amazake Chai Latte

A café-style drink that soothes you with its fragrant steam.

In a small saucepan, heat ½ cup (100 ml) of undiluted amazake, ½ cup (100 ml) of unsweetened tea and ½ teaspoon grated ginger over medium heat. In the same small saucepan, warm ¼ cup (50 ml) of milk, whisk with a milk foamer or whisk and pour into a cup. Sprinkle with cinnamon powder to taste.

Amazake Umeboshi Yuzu

The rich flavor of umeboshi plums and the citrusy kick of yuzu go great with amazake.

In a small saucepan, heat 1 scant cup (200 ml) of amazake (undiluted type) over medium heat. When warm, pour into a cup. Tear an umeboshi into pieces. Place thin slices of yuzu on top.

More Fermented Drinks

Amazake's amazing, sure, but don't forget about vinegar, salt koji and yogurt when you're concocting tasty fermented beverages. Try different recipes every day in search of your favorites.

Apple Honey Vinegar Tonic

A sweet-and-sour concoction for when you're feeling under the weather.

Place ½ of a medium-sized apple (about 5 oz/ 150 g) with the skin still on in a blender and add 3 tablespoons water and ½ tablespoons each of vinegar and honey. Pour into a glass and top with the other half of the apple, cut into cubes, if desired.

Vinegar

Vinegar

Black Vinegar Ginger Ale

The spicy ginger is tamed by the richness of black vinegar and sweetness of honey.

In a glass, combine 1 tablespoon honey, 2 teaspoons black vinegar and 2 teaspoons grated ginger. Add ice, as needed, and ⅔ cup (150 ml) of sparkling water and stir gently.

Salt Koji

Salt Koji Lemon Soda

Citric sourness with a gentle salty taste, this is great for rehydration in the summer.

Halve a lemon, cutting on of the halves into wedges and placing in the freezer. Squeeze the juice of the remaining lemon into a glass. Add 1 tablespoon honey and 1 teaspoon salt koji and mix with a spoon. Add the frozen lemon and ⅔ cup (150 ml) club soda, mixing lightly.

Peach Nectar Lassi

Thick and satisfying with a peachy sweetness!

In a blender, combine ½ cup (100 g) canned white or yellow peaches, ⅓ cup (70 g) plain yogurt, 2 tablespoons milk and 1 teaspoon lemon juice. Pulse until smooth, then pour into a glass and top with mint, if desired.

Yogurt

Carrot and Orange Vinegar Smoothie

The bright orange color makes this a perfect morning pick-me-up.

Place ½ peeled carrot (about 75 g), ⅔ cup (150 ml) orange juice and 1 teaspoon vinegar in a blender. Pulse until smooth, then pour into a glass.

Vinegar

Yogurt

Blueberry Honey Lassi

Tart blueberries and sweet honey join forces for a lassie that disappears fast!

In a blender, combine ½ cup (50 g) frozen blueberries, ½ cup (80 g) plain yogurt, ¼ cup (50 ml) milk, 1 tablespoon honey and 1 teaspoon lemon juice. Pulse until smooth, then pour into a glass. Top with additional blueberries, if desired.

Japanese Vinegar Varieties

Vinegar is a multidimensional powerhouse. Its benefits are manifold. Not only is it effective for weight loss, it promotes a clearer complexion, reduces fatigue and improves circulation since it helps limit the growth of harmful intestinal bacteria. Its contributions to cooking are evident: the bracing bite enhances flavor, meaning less salt and fewer additives are needed.

Junmai Fuji Vinegar

Pure rice vinegar from Iio Brewery in Miyazu City, Kyoto Prefecture. It is made only from rice grown without using agricultural chemicals in the local terraced rice paddies. It has not only acidity, but also a strong umami taste and a deep richness that makes dishes rich in flavor.

Iio Brewery
https://www.iio-jozo.co.jp

Sakamoto Black Vinegar

Black vinegar from Sakamoto Brewery in Kirishima City, Kagoshima Prefecture. It has a complex flavor that is different from conventional black vinegar. This is only possible with the traditional "jar brewing" method. It is a staple product that we drink every morning at home.

Sakamoto Brewery
http://www.kurozu.co.jp

Inside a Japanese Black Vinegar Brewery

Known for its depth and delicacy of flavor, Sakamoto Brewery's black vinegar is the byproduct of an ancient tradition. Made in Tsubobata (in Fukuyama-cho, Kirishima City, Kagoshima Prefecture), the sight of the jars lined up in front of the Sakurajima volcanic island is breathtaking! In these pots, the raw materials ferment, slowly becoming the black vinegar that's prized throughout Japan.

What is unusual about this operation is its outdoor location. The "jar-style" black vinegar found in Fukuyama is produced by a unique method of fermentation employed nowhere else in the world.

The ingredients couldn't be more simple: steamed rice, rice koji and groundwater. Combined in a single jar, multiple fermentation processes simultaneously occur in complex and overlapping ways to produce this prized and savored flavorant. The vinegar produced by this miraculous process is well-rounded with a complex flavor, but the principles at work behind this fermentation process are still not fully understood, adding all the more to the mystery and allure of this most flavorful of fermented foods.

Rice with a Fermented Twist

In my home, we usually add some type of fermented ingredient when making rice. It couldn't be easier, just put it in the rice cooker and let it go.

For this first recipe, Mixed-Grain Rice with Salt Koji, just add a little bit of salt koji while cooking your rice as usual (the recipe includes mixed grains, but using white rice alone is also fine). That's all you need to do to make tasty and fluffy rice; and it stays sticky and firm even after it's cooled.

I also often make rice cooked with miso. Most cooked rice dishes are flavored with salt or soy sauce, but miso can also be used by simply dissolving it in mirin or sake. It creates a rice that's rich and flavorful and keeps you coming back for more.

Miso rice goes well with root vegetables as well as mushrooms and green onions. But it's a flexible base, so add whatever you like; just give it a try!

Mixed-Grain Rice with Salt Koji

Simply adding salt koji when cooking rice gives it a deliciously salty taste and a plump texture. The stickiness remains even after the rice has cooled, making it perfect for bento lunches.

Serves 4–5

2 cups (300 g) uncooked Japanese rice
2 tablespoons multigrain rice
1 tablespoon salt koji

1 Wash the rice and drain it in a colander. Add rice and water to the inner pot of a rice cooker up to the 2-cup mark.
2 Add mixed grains and salt koji and mix well. Cook the rice as usual.

Note

The amount of water you'll need changes depending on the type of mixed grains you're using, so adjust it depending on your preferences. Of course, you can make this recipe using plain rice only!

Salt Koji

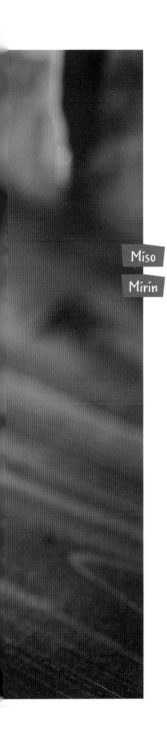

Miso

Mirin

Chicken and Burdock Miso Rice

The aroma of burdock root and the richness of chicken make this recipe a real treat. The miso adds an unexpected layer of flavor.

Serves 4–5

1½ cups (300 g) uncooked Japanese rice
1 burdock root (about 5 oz/150 g)
⅓ lb (150 g) boneless chicken breast
Thinly sliced green onion, to garnish

A ingredients:
3 tablespoons miso
2 tablespoons mirin
2 tablespoons sake

1 Rinse the rice, soak in water for 30 minutes then drain it in a colander. Mix the A ingredients together. Thinly shave the burdock root. Cut the chicken into ⅓-inch (1-cm) dice.
2 Put the soaked rice and the combined A ingredients in a rice cooker and add water up to the 2-cup level. Mix lightly. Top with the burdock root and chicken and cook using the regular setting.
3 When the rice is cooked, mix it gently with a rice paddle (**photo a**), and serve in bowls. Sprinkle with the sliced green onions.

Cherry Tomato Salt Koji Rice Pilaf

A Western-style pilaf that can be made simply by adding the ingredients to a rice cooker.

Serves 4–5

1½ cups (300 g) uncooked
  Japanese rice
½ medium onion (about 100 g)
⅛ lb (60 g) thick-cut bacon
12 cherry tomatoes
Chopped parsley, to taste
Coarsely ground black pepper

A ingredients:
1 tablespoon olive oil
1½ tablespoons salt koji
½ teaspoon grated garlic

1 Rinse the rice and soak it in water for 30 minutes, then drain it in a colander. Finely mince the onion. Cut the bacon into ⅓-inch (1-cm) dice.

2 Put the rice in a rice cooker and add water to just a little bit below the level for 2 cups. Add the A ingredients and mix lightly. Top with the onion, cherry tomatoes and bacon, and cook using the regular setting.

3 When the rice is cooked, stir it gently with a rice paddle and serve it in bowls, sprinkled with chopped parsley and coarsely ground black pepper, to taste.

Salt Koji

Mushroom and Lotus Root Miso Rice

This rich miso-flavored rice is perfect with mushrooms and your favorite root vegetables.

Serves 4–5

1½ cups (300 g) uncooked Japanese rice
1 piece lotus root (about ⅓ lb/150 g)
⅔ cup (50 g) shimeji mushrooms
⅔ cup (50 g) maitake mushrooms
1¼ cups (300 ml) dashi stock
Shredded yuzu or lemon peel, to garnish

A ingredients:
2½ tablespoons miso
1½ tablespoons mirin
1½ tablespoons sake

Miso

Mirin

1 Rinse the rice and soak it in water for 30 minutes. Combine the A ingredients.
2 Cut the unpeeled lotus root into quarters lengthwise, and then slice it into pieces ¼ inch (3 mm) thick (**photo a**). Cut off the hard root end of the shimeji mushrooms and break them into small clusters with your hands. Repeat with the maitake mushrooms, dividing them into small clusters.
3 Add the rice and the A ingredients to a rice cooker. Add the dashi stock up to the 2-cup level and mix lightly. Top it all with the lotus root, shimeji and maitake mushrooms and cook with the regular setting.
4 When the rice is cooked, stir it gently with a rice paddle and serve it in bowls, sprinkled with yuzu zest, if you have it. Lemon makes for an acceptable substitute.

a

Salt Koji

Bacon and Green Onion Salt Koji Rice

Rice packed with the umami of green onions and pork, then accented with black pepper.

Serves 4–5

1½ cups (300 g) uncooked Japanese rice
⅔ cup (150 g) thinly sliced pork belly or bacon
2 tablespoons salt koji
1 green onion
Coarsely ground black pepper, to taste

1 Rinse the rice, soak it in water for 30 minutes, then drain it in a colander. Cut the pork into 1-inch (about 3-cm) pieces, rub in half the salt koji (**photo a**) and let marinate for 10 minutes. Cut the green onion, green parts and all, into 1-inch (about 3-cm) pieces.
2 Put the drained rice in a rice cooker and add water up to the 2-cup level. Add the remaining salt koji and mix together lightly. Top it all with the pork and green onion (**photo b**) and cook using the regular setting.
3 When the rice is cooked, stir it gently with a rice paddle and serve it in bowls, sprinkled with coarsely ground black pepper, to taste.

Seasonal Rice Dishes Made with Salt Koji

I love to cook rice with seasonal ingredient. In spring, it's rice with beans and wakame seaweed. In summer, corn rice, edamame rice or tomato rice are on the menu. Then in fall, mushrooms or chestnuts dress up my rice dishes, while in winter, a range of root vegetables become the star players.

The seasoning should be suited to the ingredients, but especially for spring and summer rice dishes, I recommend using simple salt-based seasonings.

I often season corn rice and bean rice with salt koji. When you make rice dishes with salt koji, it becomes moist and sticky with a full flavor that lingers even after the dish cools—just like when you add it to plain rice.

Salt koji brings out the flavors of the ingredients and allows them to shine. Give it a try and lift your seasonal rice dishes to the next level.

Make Brown Rice More Tasty with Salt Koji

In our house, after cooking brown rice, we keep it warm in the cooker for about three days and let it rest. The resulting rice is stickier and thus easier to eat.

Using a whisk, thoroughly mix 3 cups of brown rice to help it absorb the water. Place the rice in the rice cooker and fill with water up to the 3 cups of brown rice line, then add another 2 tablespoons of water. Add adzuki beans, to taste, 1 tablespoon of salt koji, then mix lightly and cook. The key element is the salt koji! If your rice cooker has a brown rice mode, it's better use that for cooking brown rice. If not, add a tad more water when cooking brown rice.

Chapter 2

Fermentation at Every Meal

In this chapter I'll introduce you to casual recipes that make it easy to incorporate fermented fare throughout the day. It's all here: small plates, starring stir fries and menus perfect for breakfast and lunch. These are everyday dishes that you can make without any difficulty, so you can effortlessly integrate fermentation at every meal.

Easy Fermented Marinades, Pickles and Salads

Fermented foods such as salt koji, miso and amazake have their own gentle flavors, but they also have the ability to bring out the best of the ingredients they're combined with. Team players? I suppose! Just by mixing them together, they can deepen the flavor of any dish without having to use a lot of seasonings.

The first recipe I've included here, Easy Daikon Radish Pickles, is made by simply adding amazake to salt-rubbed ingredients and letting it all marinate! It's a favorite in our home, with a deliciously sweet flavor.

The leftover daikon radish peel from this dish can also be used in a kinpira stir fry. This has become one of my favorite side dishes. Just cut the daikon peel into thin strips and saute it in 1 teaspoon sesame oil. Add 1 tablespoon of mirin and 2 teaspoons of soy sauce, then sprinkle it with 1 teaspoon of white sesame seeds to finish! It becomes a surprising staple with a pleasingly crunchy texture.

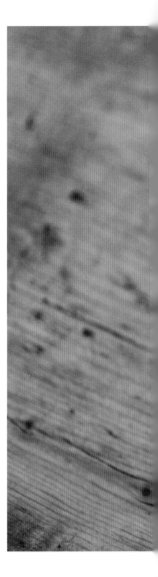

Amazake

Easy Daikon Radish Pickles

An easy side dish you can make as long as you have daikon radish and amazake.

Serves 3–4

2 cups (250 g) daikon radish
A little less than ½ cup (100 ml)
  amazake (undiluted type)
Salt, to taste
Shredded yuzu or lemon zest,
  to taste

1 Peel the daikon radish, cut it into quarters lengthwise and then cut into ½-inch (5-mm) slices. Put the sliced daikon radish in a bowl, add ½ tablespoon salt and rub it in well **(photo a)**. Let it marinate for about 10 minutes.
2 Squeeze the excess moisture out of the daikon radish and put it in a plastic bag. Add the amazake and rub it into the daikon radish through the bag **(photo b)**. Refrigerate for 30 minutes to an hour.
3 Put the daikon radish on serving plates and add the yuzu or lemon zest to taste.

Miso

Mirin

Rice Vinegar

Sesame Cucumbers with Miso & Mirin

What could be easier or more delicious than this simple and unforgettable side?

Serves 2

1 cup (140 g) cucumber
1 tablespoon ground white sesame seeds
1 teaspoon miso
1 teaspoon mirin
1 teaspoon rice vinegar
1 teaspoon sesame oil

1 Slice the cucumber thinly.
2 Mix the ground sesame seeds together with the miso, mirin, rice vinegar and sesame oil. Add the cucumber, mix together and serve.

 Note

There's just 1 unit of each ingredient in this dish! You can memorize this recipe easily, so you can make it anytime.

Salt Koji Wasabi Tomato Salad

The wasabi adds a strong accent to the richness of the salt koji. Besides being a great side dish, this also makes a nice drinking snack.

Serves 2

½ cup (100 g) tomato
1 teaspoon salt koji
Wasabi paste, to taste

1 Cut the tomato into bite-sized pieces.
2 Put the tomato in a bowl, add the salt koji and the wasabi, mix together and serve.

Note

If you don't like wasabi or you're making this for kids, you don't have to add it! You can use vinegar instead, and it will taste like a normal salad.

Salt Koji

Grilled Lotus Root Miso Sesame with Tofu Dressing

You don't need drained tofu or sesame paste for this take on classic shira-ae, vegetables with tofu sauce. It is an Enomoto family recipe.

Serves 3–4

1½ cups (200 g) lotus root
1 tablespoon olive oil
1 teaspoon soy sauce

A ingredients:
½ block (about 5 oz/150 g)
   silken tofu
3 tablespoons ground white
   sesame seeds
½ tablespoon miso
1 teaspoon sugar

1 Cut the unpeeled lotus root into quarters lengthwise, and then cut it into ½-inch (5-mm) slices. Coat the slices with the olive oil and soy sauce.
2 Line a grill with aluminum foil, spread out the lotus root slices and grill for 4 to 5 minutes on each side or until lightly browned.
3 Put the A ingredients in a bowl and combine them with a spoon until smooth. Add the cooked lotus root, mix and serve.

Note

If you don't have a grill, you can fry the lotus root pieces in a saute pan instead.

Easy Daikon Radish Kimchi

A quick kimchi that works well as a side dish as well as being a tasty drinking snack.

Serves 4–5

2½ cups (300 g) daikon radish
½ teaspoon salt

A ingredients:
2 teaspoons gochujang
2 teaspoons honey
½ teaspoon grated garlic
1 teaspoon grated ginger

1 Peel the daikon radish and cut into ⅔-inch (1.5-cm) cubes. Sprinkle with salt, rubbing it in well, and leave it to absorb for about 5 minutes. Squeeze out the excess moisture, then place the daikon radish cubes in a plastic bag.
2 Add the A ingredients to the plastic bag, squeeze out the excess air and let the contents marinate for about 30 minutes.

Note
You can refrigerate it for 2 to 3 days! This is delicious when freshly made as well as after a few days.

Gochujang

Bitter Gourd with Umeboshi and Miso

Reduce the bitterness of the gourd and make it easier to eat by blanching it quickly.

Serves 3–4

1¾ cups (250 g) bitter melon
2 umeboshi
A large pinch (4 g) katsuo-
   bushi/bonito flakes
A pinch of salt

A ingredients:
½ tablespoon miso
½ tablespoon mirin
1 teaspoon sesame oil

1 Cut the bitter gourd in half lengthwise and remove the seeds and pith with a spoon. Cut it into thin half rounds. Put the A ingredients in a large bowl and mix.
2 Bring plenty of water to a boil in a pan, add a pinch of salt and boil the bitter gourd for about 1 minute. Drain it in a colander. Cool under running water, then squeeze out the excess moisture.
3 Put the blanched bitter gourd and the katsuobushi in the bowl with the A ingredients. Pit the umeboshi, tearing them into small pieces and adding them to the bowl. Serve.

Note

If you're concerned about the alcohol in the mirin, put it into a small microwave-safe bowl and microwave uncovered for about 30 seconds to cook off the alcohol. You can refrigerate this for 3 to 4 days!

Miso   Mirin

Yogurt

Soybean Yogurt Salad

A salad with a refreshing sourness; the key is the crispy texture of the red onion.

Serves 2–3

1 cup (130 g) cooked soybeans
¼ cup (25 g) red onion
Parsley, to taste
Salt and black pepper, to taste

A ingredients:
1½ tablespoons plain yogurt
1½ tablespoons mayonnaise
A little grated garlic, to taste

1 Drain the soybeans well. Finely mince the red onion and parsley.
2 Put the soybeans, the onion, the A ingredients and a pinch each of the salt and pepper in a bowl and mix well. Serve topped with the minced parsley.

Note
If you don't have red onion, put minced regular onion in water for a while, then drain well.

Avocado and Cherry Tomato Salad with Kimchi

The creaminess of the avocado and the acidic pop of the tomatoes and kimchi form the perfect pairing.

Serves 2

½ avocado
4 cherry tomatoes
2 tablespoons napa cabbage kimchi
1 teaspoon ground white sesame seeds
1 teaspoon sesame oil
Roasted, unsalted pine nuts, to taste

1 Remove the pit and skin from the avocado and cut into bite-sized pieces. Cut the cherry tomatoes in half.
2 Put the avocado, cherry tomatoes, kimchi, ground sesame seeds and sesame oil in a bowl and gently mix. Serve topped with the roasted pine nuts, if desired.

Kimchi

Miso   Mirin   Black Rice Vinegar

Chicken Tenders and Okahijiki with Sesame Miso

This is a substantial salad combining crunchy "land seaweed" with moist, tender chicken.

Serves 2–3

½ lb (225 g) sliced boneless
   chicken breast
1 tablespoon sake
A pinch of salt
1 cup (90 g) okahijiki

A ingredients:
1 tablespoon miso
1 tablespoon black vinegar
   (or rice vinegar)
1 tablespoon ground white
   sesame seeds
1 teaspoon mirin
1 teaspoon sesame oil

1 Put the chicken pieces in a microwave-safe dish and sprinkle with the sake and salt. Cover loosely with plastic wrap and microwave for about 2 minutes 30 seconds or until just cooked. Let the pieces cool to room temperature then shred them with your hands.

2 Combine the A ingredients in a bowl. Bring plenty of water to a boil and blanch the okahijiki for about 10 seconds. Drain, then cool under running water. Cut the okahijiki into thirds and squeeze out the excess moisture.

3 Add the chicken and okahijiki to the bowl and combine.

 Note

Leave the plastic wrap on the tenders until they've cooled for a moist texture. The sauce is also delicious with cold pork or boiled vegetables. The Italian green agretti (also known as monk's beard) can replace the okahijiki; or use spinach instead for a slightly different version.

 Miso   Mirin   Rice Vinegar

Wakame Salad with Mustard Vinegar Miso Dressing

A great dish highlighting the wakame seaweed, it's also good made with broccolini.

Serves 2–3

1 tablespoon dried cut wakame seaweed
14 pieces yaki-fu (dried wheat gluten, about 10 g)
⅓ cup (50 g) cucumber
¼ teaspoon salt

A ingredients:
4 teaspoons white miso
2 teaspoons mirin
1 teaspoon rice vinegar
¼ teaspoon Japanese mustard paste

1 Soak the wakame seaweed in plenty of cold water for about 5 minutes to rehydrate it. Drain well. Rehydrate the yaki-fu the same way. Squeeze out the excess moisture by pressing each piece between your palms.
2 Slice the cucumber thinly and sprinkle the slices with the salt. Let stand for 5 minutes, then squeeze out the moisture well.
3 Put the A ingredients in a bowl and mix. Add the wakame seaweed, yaki-fu and cucumber and mix well.

Note

Adjust the amount of mustard paste to taste. If you'd prefer to remove the alcohol from the mirin, put it into a small microwave-safe bowl and microwave uncovered for about 30 seconds to cook it off.

Kabocha Squash, Mascarpone and Amazake Mash

The richness of the cheese and the tang of the amazake make this a go-to side dish.

Serves 2

⅔ cup (300 g) kabocha
   squash peeled, seeded
2 tablespoons undiluted
   amazake
2 tablespoons mascarpone
   cheese (or cream cheese)
A pinch of salt

1 Cut the kabocha squash into bite-sized pieces. Put in a microwave-safe container and cover loosely. Microwave for about 4 minutes, 30 seconds or until the squash is tender. Mash it using a potato masher or a fork while it's still hot.

2 When the squash has cooled to room temperature, add the amazake and a pinch of salt, then mix. Cool completely in the refrigerator. Then add the cheese, mix lightly and serve.

Note

If you mix the mascarpone cheese in after chilling the kabocha squash in the refrigerator, the cheese won't melt, resulting in a better consistency. This salad can be kept refrigerated for 3 to 4 days.

Amazake

Quick & Easy Fermented Stir Fries

Fermented foods can play a central role in seasoning everyday stir fries! Even with simple ingredients, the addition of fermented foods enhances the baseline of flavors, adding layers and nuance to an otherwise simple meal.

    The first recipe I included here is for a delicious stir-fried pork and cabbage blended with a dollop of miso. Just be sure not to add it to your stir fry while it's still in solid or paste form. It's difficult to make the taste uniform once the miso clings unevenly to the pork and cabbage. By simply dissolving it with mirin or sake, you can easily make a tasty, all-purpose stir-fry sauce in a well-blended dish that in the end comes cohesively together.

Pork and Cabbage with Miso

The sweet and salty miso sauce coats the pork and cabbage, creating a dish that's hard to stop eating.

Serves 2

⅔ cup (100 g) onion
2 cups (200 g) green cabbage
  leaves
½ lb (225 g) thinly sliced pork
  belly
1 teaspoon vegetable oil
4 green shiso leaves

A ingredients:
1½ tablespoons miso
2 teaspoons mirin
2 teaspoons sake

1 Cut the onion into ½-inch (5-mm) slices and the cabbage into about 1½–2 inch (4–5 cm) squares. Cut the pork into 2-inch (5-cm) pieces (**photo a**). Combine the A ingredients.

2 Heat up 1 teaspoon vegetable oil over medium heat in a skillet. Add the onion and pork and stir fry.

3 When the meat changes color, add the cabbage (**photo b**) and continue stir frying. When the cabbage is wilted, add the A ingredients and stir fry some more. Rip up the green shiso leaves and add to the stir fry.

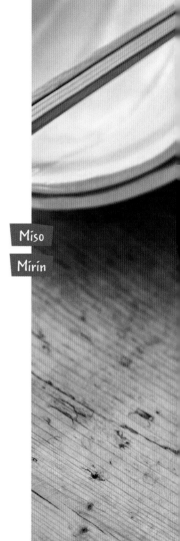

Miso

Mirin

Soy sauce is the standard go-to seasoning, but why not dilute miso with mirin to create an easy-to-use yet richly flavored sauce?

Pork and cabbage are the main ingredients in this dish, but the recipe and approach are so basic and adaptable, you can always change things up by using your favorite proteins and vegetables. Leafy greens such as bok choi and root vegetables such as carrots also go well with this dish. Chicken and salmon are delicious as alternate protein choices.

One final point to keep in mind. With fermented foods like kimchi, salt koji and black vinegar, there's no need for complicated seasonings or blends. Deep flavors are already on hand, richly imparted by those simple fermented ingredients.

Kimchi

Chicken and Kimchi Stir Fry

Another easy stir fry you can make with just a few ingredients. Add it to your regular rotation!

Serves 2

1 green onion
½ lb (250 g) boneless chicken thighs, skin on
1 teaspoon sesame oil
⅓ cup (100 g) napa cabbage kimchi

A ingredients:
1 tablespoon sake
2 teaspoons soy sauce

1 Cut the green onion into thin diagonal slices, including the green part. Cut the chicken into bite-sized pieces.
2 Heat the sesame oil over medium heat in a skillet, and put in the chicken pieces skin side down. Pan fry for about 3 to 4 minutes, then turn over and cook the other side for an additional 3 to 4 minutes.
3 When the chicken is cooked through and the juices run clear, add the green onion and kimchi and stir fry. When the green onion is wilted, add the A ingredients and stir fry briefly. Serve.

 Note

You want to crisp up the skin for more flavor, so don't move the chicken pieces around too much as you brown them!

Salt Koji Aglio Olio Mushrooms with Bacon Bits

The bacon and salt koji are an umami bomb, a nice contrast to the earthy mushrooms.

Serves 2

¾ cup (100 g) shimeji mush-
    rooms
¾ cup (100 g) maitake mush-
    rooms
1 slice bacon
1 garlic clove
1 tablespoon olive oil
1 red chili, thinly sliced
2 teaspoons salt koji
Coarsely ground black pepper

1 Trim the ends off the shimeji mushrooms and break them up into small clusters, doing the same with the maitake mushrooms. Crush the garlic clove with the side of a knife. Cut the bacon into ⅓-inch (1-cm) strips.
2 Heat the olive oil and garlic clove over medium in a skillet. Add the bacon and the two types of mushrooms to the skillet. Let them brown.
3 When the mushrooms are done, add the chili pepper slices and the salt koji and stir fry. Serve topped with a little coarsely ground black pepper.

Note

When pan frying the mushrooms, don't move them around too much or too often to intensify their umami flavors.

Sweet and Sour Pork with Black Vinegar

The richness of the black vinegar intensifies the flavors of the pork and vegetables.

Serves 2

2 small green bell peppers
⅔ cup (100 g) onion
⅔ lb (300 g) pork shoulder
Salt, to taste
Black pepper, to taste
Cornstarch or potato starch, for dredging
3 tablespoons vegetable oil

A ingredients:

2 tablespoons ketchup
1 tablespoon black vinegar
1 tablespoon soy sauce
1 tablespoon water
1 teaspoon sugar
1 teaspoon cornstarch or potato starch

1 Cut the bell peppers in half lengthwise, remove the stems and seeds, and cut roughly into chunks. Cut the onion into ⅓-inch (1-cm) slices. Cut the pork into ⅔-inch (1.5-cm) pieces. Sprinkle with a little salt and pepper and dust with cornstarch or potato starch. Mix the A ingredients together.

2 Heat the vegetable oil over medium in a skillet. Add the pork pieces and shallow fry them, turning occasionally, for 3 to 4 minutes. When the pork is cooked through, wipe out the excess oil, add the bell peppers and onion to the pan and stir fry. When the vegetables are wilted, mix again before adding the A ingredients and stir frying some more.

Note

Try using thickly cut pork for a more substantial dish or if you're serving it as an entree.

Black Vinegar

Gochujang

Beef Bulgogi with Bean Sprouts, Bell Peppers, Sesame and Gochujang

A Korean-style dish redolent with garlic and sesame oil. Don't forget to pile on the veggies!

Serves 2

2 small bell peppers
⅔ cup (100 g) onion
⅓ lb (50 g) boneless beef
⅔ cup (120 g) bean sprouts
Roasted white sesame seeds, to taste

A ingredients:
1 tablespoons soy sauce
1 tablespoon sake
1 tablespoon sesame oil
2 teaspoons sugar
2 teaspoons gochujang
1 teaspoon grated garlic

1 Cut the bell peppers in half lengthwise, remove the stems and seeds and slice thinly lengthwise. Slice the onion thinly too.
2 Put the beef, peppers and onion in a bowl, adding the A ingredients. Cover tightly with plastic wrap and let marinate for about 10 minutes.
3 Put the Step 2 ingredients and the bean sprouts in a skillet over medium-low heat. Stir fry. When the vegetables are wilted and the meat is cooked through, sprinkle with sesame seeds, to taste.

Note

By pre-seasoning the beef, bell pepper and onion, the flavors will be that much more pronounced.

The Case for Natto

My mother used to make a special natto dish for me when I was a child. She'd mix it with various ingredients such as tuna, squid, cucumber, mountain yam and takuan pickles, then add an egg and stir it all up. She'd usually make it in generous portions and serve it on a big platter at the dinner table where I loved to eat it as is or on rice or tofu.

Natto is not only rich in nutrients, it's delicious as is and is also an excellent when combined with other ingredients. It's served as part of a traditional Japanese breakfast, but it's great any time of day. So here are my family's favorites featuring this sticky delicacy for lunch or dinner.

Marinated Tuna Bomb Rice Bowl

Natto and kimchi go great together. Add marinated tuna for an even more luxurious dish!

Serves 2

¼ lb (100 g) fresh tuna sashimi

A ingredients:
1 teaspoon soy sauce
1 teaspoon mirin
1 cup (150 g) mountain yam
¼ cup (70 g) napa cabbage kimchi
1 packet (1.7 oz/50 g) natto
2 cups (500 g) hot cooked rice
2 egg yolks (optional)

Note

If you want to cook off the alcohol in the mirin, put it into a small microwave-safe bowl uncovered for about 30 seconds. This dish is also delicious made with other sashimi such as salmon or yellowtail!

1 Put the tuna sashimi in a shallow container, add the A ingredients and mix. Marinate for about 15 minutes. Peel the mountain yam and put into a ziplock plastic bag, and bash with a rolling pin into small pieces over the bag. Mix the natto with ½ of the seasoning packet the comes with it.
2 Put the hot rice in two rice bowls, top with equal amounts of the mountain yam, kimchi, natto and tuna sashimi, and slide on one egg yolk each (if using).

Natto Notes

Made from soybeans fermented with Bacillus subtillis, natto has been a favorite food of mine since childhood. I'm not alone in my love of this protein-rich powerhouse. There's a growing cohort of natto lovers out there, so there's a range of different products available. Take advantage and give it a try. Here are four I especially love!

Domestically Grown Large Bean Hime Natto

This natto is made by Sugaya Foods in Ome City, Tokyo. The soybeans are large and filling, yet very soft and easy to eat. It has a strong umami flavor and has won numerous awards from the National Natto Evaluation Committee.

Sugaya Foods
https://www.sugaya.co.jp

Domestically Grown Medium Sized Soybean Natto

This natto is made by Adumas Foods in Utsunomiya City, Tochigi Prefecture. It is often sold in supermarkets around Japan. The soybeans are on the large side of medium, with a flavor that is easy to recommend to anyone.

Adumas Foods
https://www.adumas.co.jp

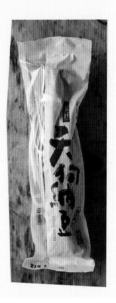

Mito Tengu Natto Tokusen Waratto Natto

This natto is made by Sasanuma Goro Shoten in Mito City, Ibaraki Prefecture. First of all, you can enjoy the visual impact of the natto wrapped in traditional straw and the pleasure of taking it out of that straw wrapping. When you open up the straw bundle, you will find dark-colored small natto grains packed tightly together. The straw gives a rich aroma to the beans, which has a complex flavor like aged red miso.

Goro Sasanuma Shoten
http://www.tengunatto.jp/

Kamakura Natto

This natto is made by Noro Foods in Kamakura, Kanagawa Prefecture. Although small in size, these beans have a strong soybean taste. Many natto sauces are sweet, but these natto sauces have a unique taste with plenty of umami from katsuobushi (bonito flakes).

Noro Foods
http://www.nattoyasan.com/

Nishijin Komachi Natto from Kyoto

This natto is from Ushiwaka Natto in Kyoto, and is made with very small soybeans. It is so stringy and sticky that it is hard to mix up, and has the most pronounced "natto" taste. This does not come with a packet of mustard as is usual with natto, but has a refreshing flavor nevertheless because the sauce is not too sweet.

Ushiwaka Natto
https://www.ushiwaka-nattou.com/

Shirasu Natto Rice Bowl

The saltiness of shirasu (boiled whitebait) and the freshness of shiso leaves, mizuna and grated daikon radish go together so well with natto! A refreshing, easy to eat Japanese.

Serves 2

2 cups (40 g) mizuna greens
2 green shiso leaves
1 packet (1.7 oz/50 g) natto
2 cups (500 g) hot cooked rice
1½ tablespoons shirasu
  (boiled whitebait)
Grated daikon radish, to taste
Soy sauce, to taste

1 Cut the mizuna greens into 1- to 1½-inch (3–4 cm) pieces. Finely julienne the green shiso leaves. Add half of the included sauce packet to the natto and mix well.

2 Put the hot rice into two bowls and top with equal amounts of mizuna greens, shirasu and natto. Add equal amounts of drained grated daikon radish and green shiso leaves. Drizzle with soy sauce and serve.

Note

The shirasu is salty, so adjust the amount of soy sauce to taste. Mix well before eating.

Natto

Natto Carbonara Udon

Natto adds a creamy richness to this healthy yet substantial dish.

Serves 2

2 eggs
Green onions, to taste
2 packets (9 oz/250 g each) frozen udon noodles
Nori seaweed, to taste

A ingredients:
2 packets (1.7 oz/50 g each) natto
2 tablespoons grated Parmesan cheese
1 tablespoon soy sauce
1 teaspoon mirin

1 Break the eggs into a large bowl, and beat well. Add the A ingredients and mix well. Slice the green onions thinly.
2 Cook the frozen udon noodles following the instructions on the packet. Add the hot udon noodles to the Step 1 bowl, mix and serve topped with the green onion and ripped-up nori seaweed.

Note

By beating the eggs and mixing the natto well, the sauce will have a smooth, creamy texture. If you want to cook off the alcohol in the mirin, put it into a small microwave-safe bowl and microwave uncovered for about 30 seconds.

Natto   Mirin

Fermented Foods for Busy Mornings

Some days we have rice in the morning, but most days we have bread instead. Bread, made with yeast, is of course a fermented food too. So it pairs perfectly with other fermented fare. I enjoy combining bread with a variety of fermented ingredients to give me an extra dose of the fuel I need to get through a busy day.

What I make most often is perhaps the simplest: miso toast. All you have to do is spread white miso on bread and toast it. Add butter and you have a very tasty treat. To take it to another level, you can mix chopped green onions with some white miso to make the Green Onion Miso Toast featured on page 66.

For another option, you can mix salt koji and yogurt and use it like mayonnaise. Spread it on bread, add some ham slices and you're got a totally tasty sandwich. Yogurt and honey can be combined and used as a substitute for whipped cream. I spread it on bread and top it with seasonal fruits for an old-school Japanese fruit sandwich. Give it a try, and I'm sure you'll be hooked.

Natto goes surprisingly well with bread too. I love to put takuan pickles on natto toast. The acidic pop and crunchy texture are the ideal accent. I also like to add natto to toasted bread with melted cheese finished off with some torn green shiso leaves and nori seaweed. I also made bread quiche on days when I have a little extra time. Simply hollow out the bread a little, add your favorite ingredients and a beaten egg and toast it at low heat.

 Natto

Natto Cheese Toast

Natto with rice is standard, but those fermented soybeans go surprisingly well with bread too!

Serves 2

2 packets (1.7 oz/50 g each) natto
1½ tablespoons chopped takuan pickles
Drizzle of olive oil
2 slices sandwich bread (whole wheat, if possible)
½ cup (70 g) shredded pizza cheese
Green shiso leaves, to serve
Olive oil, to serve

1 Put the natto, the sauce packet that comes with it and the chopped takuan pickles in a bowl and mix well.
2 Drizzle a little olive oil on each of the bread slices, and spread with the Step 1 mixture and equal amounts of the cheese.
3 Crumple up a sheet of aluminum foil and place it on the rack of a toaster oven. Place the bread slices from Step 2 on top. Toast until browned for 6 to 7 minutes. Serve topped with torn green shiso leaves.

Note

Whole wheat bread will have a nuttier flavor when toasted. By using crumpled-up aluminum foil, the bottom of the bread will get nicely toasted without becoming soggy. If you don't have green shiso leaves, use some minced green onion to top these instead.

Green Onion Miso Toast

Miso mixed with green onion is a surprisingly simple and terrifically tasty topping for bread!

Serves 2

2 tablespoons white miso
1 tablespoon finely sliced green onion
2 slices bread
Butter, to taste

1 Mix the white miso and green onion together (**photo a**).
2 Spread the mixture on the bread slices (**photo b**) and toast in a toaster oven until browned for 3 to 4 minutes.
3 Serve topped with some butter.

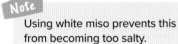

Note

Using white miso prevents this from becoming too salty.

Salt Koji Yogurt Ham Sandwich

Add salt koji to plain yogurt for a mayonnaise substitute. It's great in sandwiches!

Serves 2

¼ cup (60 g) strained or Greek yogurt
2 teaspoons salt koji
2 slices bread of your choice (such as ciabatta)
2 leaves lettuce
2–3 slices deli ham

1 Mix the yogurt and salt koji together.
2 Toast the bread of your choice until crispy. Spread half the Step 1 mixture onto one piece, then the rest onto the other piece and cut them both in half. Top with the lettuce and ham and the remaining bread.

Note
You can also spread the yogurt and salt koji mixture on toasted baguette slices.

How to make strained yogurt
Place a colander on top of a bowl, line with a paper towel and spoon in plain yogurt. Cover with plastic wrap and refrigerate overnight.
■ You'll end up with half the plain yogurt in weight: (4 oz/120 g becomes 2 oz/60 g) in strained yogurt.

Lotus Root and Onion Bacon Quiche Toast

A bread quiche you can make easily in a toaster oven. The lotus root makes it fun to eat.

Serves 2

¼ lotus root
⅓ cup (50 g) onion
2 slices bacon
1½ tablespoons shredded
   pizza cheese
2 thick slices bread

A ingredients:
½ teaspoon miso
3 tablespoons whole milk
2 eggs
1 tablespoon grated Parmesan
   cheese

Note

If it looks like the toast is browning too fast, cover the top with another sheet of aluminum foil.

1 Cut the unpeeled lotus root into quarters lengthwise, and cut into ¼-inch (3-mm) slices. Put the sliced lotus root into a bowl of water. Cut the onion in half and then into thin slices (**photo a**). Cut the bacon into ⅓-inch (1-cm) pieces.

2 Place the lotus root and bacon pieces in a microwave-safe container and cover loosely with plastic wrap. Microwave for about 1 minute 30 seconds.

3 Put the miso in a bowl, add the milk and mix well. Add the egg and grated Parmesan cheese and mix.

4 Press down inside the bread crusts to make an indentation on the slices (**photo b**). Distribute half the lotus root, onion, bacon and shredded pizza cheese equally between the bread slices and top with the A mixture. Divide the rest of the lotus root equally between the slices.

5 Crumple up a sheet of aluminum foil and place it on the toaster oven rack. Place the bread slices from Step 4 on the foil. Toast for about 15 minutes until browned and serve.

Miso

 Yogurt

Fruit-Topped Honey Yogurt Toast

Combine honey with yogurt to make an easy whipped cream substitute. This is a homemade version of the type of sweet sandwich that's very popular in Japan.

Serves 2

¼ cup (60 g) strained or Greek yogurt (see page 67)
½ tablespoon honey
2 slices bread
Fresh fruit of your choice

1 Combine the yogurt and honey.
2 Toast the sliced bread until it's crispy, spread with the Step 1 mix and top with fresh fruit of your choice.

Note

This combination of yogurt and honey is a convenient substitute for whipped cream when you just want a small amount. You may even prefer its more refreshing taste! Any seasonal fresh fruit goes well with this sandwich. I also recommend using kiwi, mango or blueberries.

Amazake Scrambled Eggs

The gentle sweetness of amazake is the secret to these deliciously fluffy scrambled eggs.

Serves 2

2 eggs
2 tablespoons undiluted
  amazake
A pinch of salt
2 teaspoons butter
1 cup (50 g) salad greens
4 cherry tomatoes, halved
4 slices toasted baguette

1 Beat the eggs in a bowl, add the amazake and pinch of salt, and mix.
2 Heat the butter in a skillet over medium. Add the egg mixture from Step 1 and mix. When the eggs are cooked as you desire, transfer to plates and serve with the lettuce, cherry tomatoes and baguette.

Amazake

Vegetable-Packed Salt Koji Soup

A simple, nourishing soup that you'll want to have every day.

Serves 2

2 cabbage leaves (about 3 oz/100 g)
⅓ cup (50 g) onion
⅓ cup (50 g) carrot
1 cup (60 g) broccoli florets
1 slice bacon
1½ tablespoons salt koji
2 teaspoons olive oil
Coarsely ground black pepper

1 Cut the cabbage into easy-to-eat pieces. Cut the onion into the same size pieces, as well as the unpeeled carrot. Cut the bacon into ⅓-inch (1-cm) pieces.

2 Heat the olive oil in a pan over medium. Saute the onion, carrot and bacon. When the onion is wilted, add the cabbage and broccoli and saute quickly. Add 2 cups (500 ml) water and the salt koji. Bring to a boil, simmer for about 2 minutes, and ladle into bowls. Season to taste with coarsely ground black pepper.

Salt Koji

Note

Other vegetables such as celery and potatoes work in this soup too, as do canned or frozen beans of your choice such as kidney beans or chickpeas.

Chapter 3

Fermentation for Life

It's easy to see how fermentation can move beyond mere food to become a lifestyle. That's why I'm inspired by fermented foods and the pathways they pave to a healthier life. The all-purpose sauces, dressings and marinades collected here typify the essence of fermented finesse. They showcase the power, punch and piquancy of these all-purpose superfoods.

All-Purpose Fermented Sauces

These recipes for sauces made with fermented products are as convenient as they are scrumptious! Just make them in advance, then they'll be on hand in the fridge, perfect for a wide range of dishes including salads, steamed vegetables and meats.

Try the Amazake Sesame Miso Sauce and Fragrant Black Vinegar Ginger Sesame Sauce for chilled summer dishes. Gochujang Miso Honey Sauce and Salt Koji Lemon Honey Dressing are great with dumplings and fried foods. Spicy Kimchi Sesame Soy Sauce adds the perfect pop to cold tofu, and Ginger Miso Sesame Sauce is an ideal accompaniment to steamed fish.

Try these sauces with your everyday dishes, and you'll be surprised how frequently you turn to them for their fantastic fermented flavors.

Gochujang Miso Honey Sauce

Put 2 tablespoons each of gochujang and honey in a bowl and add 1 tablespoon each of miso, soy sauce and vinegar. Mix well.

`Gochujang` `Miso`

Amazake Sesame Miso Sauce

Put 4 tablespoons undiluted amazake, 2 tablespoons ground sesame seeds and 2 teaspoons each miso and black vinegar in a bowl and mix together.

`Salt Koji` **STORAGE TIME: All the sauces can be stored in a container and refrigerated for 3–4 days.**

Salt Koji Lemon Honey Dressing

Put the juice of one lemon (about 2 tablespoons and 2 teaspoons), 2 tablespoons each of salt koji and olive oil and 1 tablespoon of honey in a bowl and mix together.

`Salt Koji`

Ginger Miso Sesame Sauce

Put 2 tablespoons of mirin in a small microwave-safe bowl, and cook uncovered for about 1 minute to burn off the alcohol. Add 1½ tablespoons rice vinegar, 1 tablespoon each of miso and sesame oil and 1 tablespoon grated ginger to the bowl and mix together.

`Mirin` `Miso` `Rice Vinegar`

Spicy Kimchi Sesame Soy Sauce

Put 1 tablespoon of mirin in a small microwave-safe bowl, and cook uncovered for about 40 seconds to burn off the alcohol. Chop up ¼ cup (60 g) of napa cabbage kimchi roughly and add it to the bowl. Add 2 teaspoons of sesame oil and 1 teaspoon of soy sauce and mix together.

`Mirin` `Kimchi`

Fragrant Black Vinegar Ginger Sesame Sauce

Finely mince 4 inches (10 cm) of green onion and put it in a bowl. Add 2 tablespoons each of soy sauce and black vinegar, 1 tablespoon of sesame oil, 2 teaspoons of sugar and 1 teaspoon of grated ginger and mix together.

`Black Vinegar`

Ginger Miso Sesame Sauce
The richness of miso and the refreshing flavor of ginger add nice accents to this sauce.

Gochujang Miso Honey Sauce
A deeply flavored, spicy sauce with the sweetness of gochujang and honey.

Salt Koji Lemon Honey Dressing
The acidic pop of lemon and the deep flavor of salt koji are a perfect match.

Fragrant Black Vinegar Sauce
An all-purpose sauce that combines the crunch of green onion with tangy black vinegar.

Amazake Sesame Miso Sauce
Combines the gentle sweetness of amazake with the richness of sesame.

Spicy Kimchi Sesame Soy Sauce
A spicy sauce with the fun crunchy texture of kimchi.

Flavor Packed Fermented Salad Dressings

Tomato, Bell Pepper & Salt Koji Salsa is great with hot dogs or crispy grilled pork, while Soy, Honey & Black Vinegar Dressing is a perfect condiment for hamburgers or as a topping for chicken. Pair the Vegetable, Egg & Yogurt Relish with fried foods, while the classic Carrot & Onion Honey Dressing is a refrigerator staple for an impromptu salad or as a topping for roasted root vegetables. Fermented salad dressings are a great way to double up on the veggies while enhancing the flavors in every forkful.

Rice Vinegar   Salt Koji

Salt Koji   Rice Vinegar

Tomato, Bell Pepper & Salt Koji Salsa

Makes just less than 1 cup (200 ml)

STORAGE TIME: Can be stored in a container and refrigerated for 2 to 3 days.

Cut half a tomato (about 3 oz/100 g) into ⅓-inch (1-cm) dice. Cut a quarter yellow bell pepper into ⅓-inch (1-cm) pieces. Finely mince ¼ onion (about 2 oz/60 g). Put all the vegetables into a bowl. Add 1 tablespoon olive oil, 2 teaspoons each salt koji and lemon juice, and grated garlic and red chili pepper flakes, to taste, to the bowl and mix.

Note

Enjoy the fresh flavor and texture of chunky vegetables! Also great served on panfried chicken or pork.

Carrot & Onion Honey Dressing

Makes about 1¼ cups (300 ml)

STORAGE TIME: Can be refrigerated for up to a week in a storage container.

Chop up 1 small carrot (about 5 oz/150 g) and ½ onion (about 3 oz/100 g) roughly and put them into a blender. Add 2 tablespoons and 2 teaspoons each of olive oil and rice vinegar to the blender plus 2 tablespoons honey, 2 teaspoons light soy sauce and ¼ teaspoon salt. Blend until smooth.

Note

If you don't have a blender, grate the carrot and onion, add the seasonings and mix it all up with a whisk. You don't need to peel the carrot.

Yogurt

Vegetable, Egg & Yogurt Relish

Great served on fried fish or filets lightly sauteed in olive oil.

Makes just less than 1 cup (200 ml)

Cut ½ of a small (or ¼ of a large) cucumber into ⅓-inch (1-cm) dice. Cut a quarter red bell pepper into ⅓-inch (1-cm) dice. Sprinkle the cucumber with a little salt, rub it in and let stand for 5 minutes. Wrap it in paper towels and squeeze out the excess moisture. Finely mince ⅛ red onion (about 1 oz/25 g). Roughly chop a hard-boiled egg. Put the cucumber, bell pepper, red onion, hard-boiled egg, 5 tablespoons plain yogurt, 1 tablespoon olive oil, 2 pinches salt and a little black pepper in a bowl and mix.

Note

Rubbing salt into the cucumber and squeezing it out prevents the dressing from becoming too watery. Since this dressing is packed with vegetables and becomes watery quickly, use it up as soon as you make it.

Soy, Honey & Black Vinegar Dressing

Makes just less than 1 cup (200 ml)

STORAGE TIME: Can be refrigerated in a container for 3 to 4 days.

Mince ½ onion (about 3 oz/100 g) finely, place in a microwave-safe bowl, cover loosely and microwave for about 1 minute. Add 1 tablespoon soy sauce, 2 tablespoons black vinegar, 2 tablespoons olive oil and 1 tablespoon honey and mix together.

Black Vinegar

Fermentation for Dinner

Fermented foods are made for marinades. The process is so easy, all it takes is a scrumptious marinade paired with one of your favorite foods to convince you.

Pickling liquid and fermented marinades can be delicious on their own. Their deep flavors bring out the best in the ingredients, so additional seasonings aren't needed. Not only do marinades add layers of flavor, they also tenderize meat and fish by breaking down the proteins, making them easier to digest and increasing their nutritional value.

In particular, the Salt Koji Marinated Pork and Amazake Char Siu Roast Pork, which use larger cuts of meat, are dishes that should be marinated slowly to experience the tenderness and depth of flavor fermented marinades impart.

1. Fermented foods make delicious marinades.
They impart umami and sweetness while allowing you to reduce the amounts of salt and sugar you're using.

2. The power of enzymes transforms and tenderizes meat and fish.
The enzymes contained in some fermented foods help to break down proteins and make meats and fish more tender.

3. Fermented foods pump up the nutritional value.
Fermented foods themselves are rich in fiber, vitamins and other nutrients. Using fermented foods not only makes other ingredients tasty but also increases their nutritional value.

Amazake

Amazake Chicken Teriyaki

A teriyaki you can make without sugar; highlight instead the distinct sweetness of amazake.

Serves 2

STORAGE TIME: The marinated chicken from Step 1 can be refrigerated for 3 to 4 days or frozen for a month.

¾ lb (300 g) boneless chicken thighs, skin on
3 tablespoons undiluted amazake
1½ tablespoons soy sauce
2 teaspoons vegetable oil
Baby lettuce leaves, to taste

Note
Since amazake burns easily, cover the pan and cook the chicken slowly over low heat.

1 Poke several holes into the skin side of the chicken thighs with a fork and place them in a plastic bag. Add the amazake and 1½ tablespoons soy sauce. Refrigerate overnight.
2 Heat the vegetable oil in a skillet over medium. Turn the heat down to low, then add the chicken, skin side down (reserve the marinade). Cover with a lid and cook until browned for about 5 minutes.
3 Turn the chicken over, cover the skillet again and cook for a further 5 to 6 minutes to cook through thoroughly.
4 Remove the lid and wipe out the excess fat in the skillet with paper towels. Add the reserved marinade from Step 2, turn the heat to high and turn the chicken over several times to coat it with the sauce (**photo a**). Take the chicken out of the skillet and let it rest for 5 minutes or so. Cut it into easy-to-eat pieces, and serve with a handful of baby lettuce leaves.

a

Steamed Salmon and Mushrooms with Miso

A newfound favorite? This sweet, rich miso marinade certainly makes the case.

Serves 2

2 boneless salmon filets
1 cup (100 g) cabbage leaves
¾ cup (100 g) maitake mushrooms
¾ cup (100 g) shimeji mushrooms

A ingredients:
1½ tablespoons miso
1½ tablespoons mirin
2 teaspoons sake

1 Put the A ingredients in a plastic bag and mix. Add the salmon pieces (**photo a**) and refrigerate for about 15 minutes. Cut the cabbage leaves into about 1–1½ inch (3–4 cm) pieces. Cut off the root ends of the shimeji mushrooms and break into small clumps, then do the same with the maitake mushrooms.
2 Spread out the cabbage in a skillet and place the salmon pieces on top. Surround the salmon pieces with the mushrooms. Pour in the marinade left in the plastic bag. Cover the skillet and heat over medium.
3 When steam starts coming out of the skillet turn down the heat to low. Cook for about 15 minutes, then serve right away.

Note

You can use Spanish mackerel or swordfish instead of the salmon. Storage time: The marinated salmon from Step 1 can be refrigerated for 2 to 3 days or frozen for 1 month.

Miso   Mirin

Salt Koji Marinated Pork

A convenient dish, just boil and eat or you always can grill or stirfry it with vegetables!

Serves 2

STORAGE TIME: Refrigerate for up to 3 to 4 days or up to 1 month in the freezer.

1 lb 2 oz (500 g) pork shoulder
2½ tablespoons salt koji

Poke holes all over the pork with a fork, then place in a plastic bag. Add the salt koji, rubbing it in thoroughly. Squeeze out as much air as possible from the bag and refrigerate for 2 days.

Salt Koji

Note

You can also marinate pork belly the same way.

Simmered Salt Koji Pork

Highlighting the Power of Salt Koji!

Serves 2–3

Put the salt-koji-marinated pork in a heavy pan with all the salt koji used to marinate it. Add enough water to cover the meat (4¼– 6⅓ cups/1–1.5 liters) and heat over medium. When the pan comes to a boil, skim the surface turn the meat over and adjust the heat to low, cooking for 12 to 13 minutes. Turn the meat over again, then turn off the heat. Cover the pan and let it stand for about 90 minutes to cool. Cut into ⅓-inch (1-cm) slices and serve with the vegetables and garnishes of your choice.

Salt Koji

a

Note

By cooking the pork using residual heat, it'll become tender and moist. It's also delicious sliced and panfried in an oiled pan with various garnishes!

Salt koji | Black vinegar, Vinegar

Salt Koji Hainanese Chicken Rice

No dry chicken here, this dish stays moist and juicy when cooked with salt koji!

a

Serves 3–4

STORAGE TIMES: The chicken can be refrigerated at the Step 1 phase for 3 to 4 days or frozen for up to a month.

1 lb 2 oz (500 g) boneless chicken thighs
2 tablespoons salt koji
1½ cups (300 g) uncooked Japanese rice
1 garlic clove, peeled
A 1-inch (2.5-cm) piece ginger
The green part of a green onion

For the Green Onion Sauce:
4 inches (10 cm) finely minced green onion
2 tablespoons Thai fish sauce (nam pla)
2 tablespoons black vinegar or rice vinegar
2 teaspoons sugar
2 teaspoons sesame oil
2 teaspoons water

Fresh coriander, to serve
Lemon wedges, to serve
1 tablespoon sake

1 Put the chicken in a plastic bag. Add the salt koji and rub it in, and refrigerate for at least an hour or overnight.

2 Rinse the rice and soak it for 30 minutes, and drain in a colander. Cut the garlic clove in half. Slice the ginger thinly with the skin on. Cut the fresh coriander leaves into easy to eat pieces (keep the roots in reserve). Cut the lemon into wedges.

3 Put the rice and sake into a rice cooker and add water up to the 2-cup level. Put the chicken and salt koji in the rice cooker and add the garlic, ginger, the green part of a green onion and some of the coriander roots (photo a). Cook using the regular setting. Combine the Green Onion Sauce ingredients.

4 When the rice is cooked, take the ingredients other than the rice from the cooker and mix up the rice. Cut the chicken into easy-to-eat pieces. Put the rice, chicken and the fresh coriander leaves into serving bowls and serve accompanied with lemon wedges.

Note

The Green Onion Sauce can be used on its own or poured over vegetables to make a salad or as a condiment for thick fried tofu. Even though chicken cooked in this way tends to become dry, by marinating it beforehand in salt koji, it'll become juicy and tender.

Tender Amazake Ginger Pork

The amazake tenderizes the meat and proves the perfect pairing with the ginger.

Serves 2

STORAGE TIME: The pork can be refrigerated in the Step 1 for half a day or frozen for up to a month.

½ lb (225 g) thinly sliced pork
  shoulder
½ medium onion
2 large cabbage leaves
3 green shiso leaves
2 teaspoons vegetable oil

For the Marinade:
3 tablespoons undiluted amazake
1½ tablespoons soy sauce
2 teaspoons grated ginger

1 Make shallow cuts across the surface of the pork pieces and place them in a shallow container. Combine the Marinade ingredients, add it to the container and marinate the pork for 30 minutes to an hour in the refrigerator. Cut the onion into ½ inch (5-mm) slices. Shred the cabbage and shiso leaves and distribute them evenly among serving plates.

2 Add the vegetable oil to a skillet and heat over medium. Add the onion and stir fry. When the onion is wilted, turn the heat down to medium-low, lightly drain the pork and spread the pieces in the skillet (reserve the marinating liquid). When the meat has changed color, take it out right away and put on the serving plates from Step 1.

3 Add the reserved marinating liquid from Step 2 to the skillet and heat it through. When it comes to a boil, pour it over the pork and serve.

Note

The key to keeping the meat tender is to take it out of the skillet as soon as it's changed color!

Amazake

Crispy Fried Tuna with Mountain Yam, Salt Koji and Ginger

Salt koji tenderizes the yellowtail and mountain yam, which are then crisply deep fried: Yes, yes, yes!

Serves 2

STORAGE TIME: The mountain yam and yellowtail can be refrigerate in the Step 1 state for 3 to 4 days.

½ lb (220 g) yellowtail tuna
1 cup (150 g) mountain yam
1 sudachi citrus or lime
Cornstarch or potato starch, for dredging
Vegetable oil, for deep frying

A ingredients:
2 tablespoons salt koji
1 teaspoon grated garlic

1 Wash the unpeeled mountain yam well, and cut it up roughly. Cut each piece of yellowtail into thirds. Put the mountain yam, yellowtail and the A ingredients into a plastic bag (**photo a**) and refrigerate for about 15 minutes. Cut the sudachi or lime in half horizontally.
2 Pat the mountain yam and yellowtail dry, then dust the pieces with potato starch or cornstarch.
3 Put about ⅓ inch (1 cm) of vegetable oil in a frying and pan and heat over medium. Put the yellowtail and mountain yam pieces in the oil and deep fry for about 4 to 5 minutes while turning often (**photo b**). Drain off the oil and serve with the sudachi or lime.

Salt Koji

Amazake

Amazake Char Siu Roast Pork

Amazingly tender char siu pork can be made easily in a skillet.

Serves 2–3

STORAGE TIME: The pork can be refrigerated for 3 to 4 days (in the Step 1 state) or frozen for a month.

1 lb 2 oz (500 g) pork shoulder
4 tablespoons undiluted amazake
1 tablespoon vegetable oil

For the Marinade:
3 tablespoons tian mian jiang (Chinese sweet bean paste)
2 tablespoons soy sauce
3 thin slices ginger
Green part of a green onion
1 star anise

1 Poke holes all over the pork with a fork (**photo a**). Put the meat into a plastic bag. Add the amazake and rub it in. Add the Marinade ingredients and rub. Eliminate as much air as possible and refrigerate for at least an hour or overnight.

2 Take the marinated pork out of the refrigerator an hour before cooking time. Heat the vegetable oil in a skillet over medium, drain off the pork and put it in the skillet (reserve the marinating liquid). Panfry the pork for about 3 minutes while turning it to brown it all over.

3 Add ½ cup (100 ml) water plus the reserved marinating liquid to the skillet. Bring it to a boil, then turn the heat down to low. Simmer, covered, for 8 to 9 minutes. Turn over the meat, and simmer for another 8 to 9 minutes.

4 Transfer the pork with the cooking liquid to a storage container (**photo b**) and let it cool. Slice it thinly and serve it with the garnishes of your choice.

Note

Since the pork will continue absorbing the flavors from the cooking liquid as it cools, I recommend using a storage container that fits the size of the meat. If you don't have a container that's the right size, you can put the cooking liquid and pork in a plastic bag to cool instead.

Amazake Chicken Curry with Colorful Vegetables

The amazake tenderizes the chicken, and the miso brings out the umami of the vegetables.

Serves 2

STORAGE TIME: The chicken can be refrigerated for 3 to 4 days (in the Step 1 state) or frozen for up to a month.

⅔ lb (300 g) boneless chicken thighs

3 tablespoons undiluted amazake

2 tablespoons curry powder

¼ each medium yellow and red bell peppers

2 okra

1 cup (250 g) eggplant

1 medium-sized white onion

1 cup (200 g) whole tomatoes

1 teaspoon grated garlic

2 teaspoons grated ginger

2 cups (500 g) hot cooked rice (mixed-grain rice if possible)

¼ teaspoon salt

Black pepper, to taste

4 tablespoons olive oil

1 tablespoon miso

1 Cut the chicken into bite-sized pieces and season them with the salt and pepper. Rub the seasonings into the chicken, then put the chicken into a plastic bag. Add the amazake and curry powder and rub it in (**photo a**). Refrigerate overnight.

2 Roughly chop the bell peppers. Trim the okra and cut them in half lengthwise. Cut the eggplant into quarters. Finely mince the onion.

3 Heat 2 tablespoons of olive oil in a skillet over medium-high. Add the bell peppers, okra and eggplant and stir fry. When the vegetables are lightly browned, remove them.

4 Add 2 more tablespoons of olive oil to the skillet and heat over medium. Add the onion and stir fry. When the onion is lightly browned, push it to one side of the skillet and add the chicken and marinade. Brown the chicken on both sides (**photo b**).

5 Add the garlic and ginger and stir fry until fragrant. Crush the canned whole tomatoes, add them the skillet with the liquid and continue stir frying. When the tomatoes are soft and blended, add ½ cup (100 ml) water and 1 tablespoon of miso and mix them in (**photo c**). Turn the heat down to medium-low and cover the skillet.

6 Simmer while stirring occasionally for 7 to 8 minutes. Arrange on plates with the rice and top with the Step 3 vegetables.

Note

By browning the vegetables and chicken properly, you'll really bring out the flavors. Give it a taste, and if it lacks flavor, add a bit more miso.

Miso
Amazake

More Easy Fermentation Recipes

These recipes embody the ease and flexibility fermented foods are famous for. What could be simpler than just marinate and eat! These recipes are great as side dishes or drinking snacks, so don't be surprised if they make frequent appearances at your weekend gatherings and midweek meals

Salt koji

Salt Koji Tofu

A dish that has just the right amount of saltiness, it really whets your appetite.

Serves 2

STORAGE TIME: The tofu can be refrigerated for 3 to 4 days in the Step 1 state.

⅓ block (5 oz/150 g) silken tofu
1 tablespoon salt koji

1 Line a shallow container with paper towels, spread on half the salt koji, then put the tofu on top. Spread the rest of the salt koji on top of the tofu and wrap the tofu with the paper towels.
2 Wrap the tofu with plastic wrap (**photo a**) and refrigerate overnight. Cut into easy-to-eat pieces.

Note
The tofu may fall apart easily, so wrap it very gently.

Miso-Marinated Egg Yolks

Simple is best. Just add the egg yolks to the mirin and miso mixture and enjoy!

Serves 2

STORAGE TIME: The egg yolks can be refrigerated for 4 to 5 days.

2 very fresh or pasteurized
  egg yolks
2 teaspoons mirin
4 tablespoons miso

1 Break the eggs into a bowl and scoop out the egg yolks with a spoon (**photo a**).
2 Put the mirin in a small microwave-safe bowl and cook for about 30 seconds uncovered to cook off the alcohol. Add the miso and mix well.
3 Put half of the Step 2 mixture into two small containers. Top each with thick paper towels, make an indent (**photo b**) and slide the egg yolks into the indents.
4 Spread the remaining Step 2 mixture on thick paper towels and place them on top of the egg yolks (**photo c**). Cover the containers with plastic wrap and refrigerate for 2 to 3 days.

Miso Mirin

a

b

c

Note
  The yolks are ready to eat in 2 to 3 days. If you want an even richer taste, marinate them for a few more days.

Chapter 4

Make-Ahead Refrigerated Recipes

These make-ahead miracles are your unbeatable allies on busy days. From soboro (minced meat dishes) to simple side dishes you can quickly transform into marquee-name entrees, it's always ideal to have these tricks up your culinary sleeves! Incorporate this flavorful fermented fare into your bento boxes or side dishes. But watch out, you just might become a fermentation master if you do!

Isn't it convenient to have some premade dishes already stashed in the refrigerator? We're only a two-person family, so I don't want to make too many items in advance and then feel pressured to use them up. So I make a smaller amount of these key staples and am always glad to have them on hand.

Crunchy Pickled Cucumbers are a must during the summer months. Many people have made this popular preparation from my YouTube and Instagram posts, and it's not surprising to learn it's one of my personal favorites. The crunchy texture of the cucumbers is so addictive that you can't stop eating them. It's also great when you give it a slightly spicy twist.

Yogurt Potato Salad is another hit in our household. I make this dish without any mayonnaise, using healthy yogurt and olive oil instead. Even my husband, a major mayo fan, loves this dish. It always disappears whenever I have some left over in the refrigerator. Maybe I should double the amount?

Here I'll show you how to make several other easy in-advance dishes for bentos, sudden snacks or unexpected guests.

Amazake

Amazake Soboro Rice Topping

A slightly sweet ground chicken dish that uses no sugar.

Serves 2

½ lb (220 g) ground chicken
⅓ cup (80 ml) undiluted amazake
2 teaspoons minced ginger
1½ tablespoons soy sauce

1 Put the ground chicken, amazake, ginger and soy sauce in a pan and mix well.
2 Heat over medium, while stirring, until there's no moisture left in the pan and the chicken has turned color.

Note

By mixing the ingredients together before starting to cook, the chicken will be more tender and not clump up as much. The chicken tends to stick together at the beginning, so mix it quickly.

Soft-Set Scrambled Egg Soboro Rice Bowl

Serves 2

Fill two rice bowls with hot rice. Put 2 beaten eggs, 2 tablespoons undiluted amazake and ½ teaspoon soy sauce in a bowl and mix together. Heat up 2 teaspoons of butter in a skillet over medium. Pour the egg mixture into the skillet and stir. When the eggs are soft set, place them on top of the rice in the rice bowls. Top with Amazake Soboro and some nozawana pickles.

Eat it like this

Amazake

Note

Amazake is used in both the egg mixture and the soboro, so the sweetness balance is just right.

Black Vinegar

Crunchy Pickled Cucumbers

This dish allows you to enjoy lots of crunchy cucumbers. You'll have a hard time stopping!

Serves 4–5

STORAGE TIME: This can be refrigerated for 4 to 5 days.

2⅔ cups (400 g) cucumbers
1½ teaspoons coarse salt

A ingredients:
2 tablespoons soy sauce
2 tablespoons black vinegar
4 teaspoons sugar
2 teaspoons sesame seeds
2 red chili peppers, thinly sliced

Note
Use water bottles as weights!

1 Slice the cucumbers into ½-inch (5-mm) rounds. Put them in a bowl, sprinkle on the coarse salt and rub it in well. Transfer the cucumbers to a plastic bag, top with a heavy weight (**photo a**) and refrigerate for at least an hour or overnight.
2 Squeeze out the excess moisture from the cucumbers, then wrap them in paper towels and squeeze them out some more. Place in a microwave-safe storage container.
3 Put the A ingredients in a small pan over medium heat and bring to a boil. Add to the container with the cucumbers from Step 2 and let cool, then refrigerate.

Salt Koji Chicken Tenders

By simply rubbing the chicken tenders with salt koji, they become moist and delicious, fit for a feast.

Serves 2

STORAGE TIME: Refrigerate the chicken tenders immersed in the cooking liquid for 3–4 days.

½ lb (225 g) boneless chicken tenders
1 tablespoon salt koji
1 tablespoon olive oil
Radish sprouts, to taste

1 Put the chicken tenders in a plastic bag. Add the salt koji and rub it in (**photo a**). Refrigerate for at least 30 minutes or overnight.
2 Put 3 cups (700 ml) of water in a pan and heat over medium. When it comes to a boil, add the olive oil and the chicken tenders with the salt koji, then turn the heat off (**photo b**).
3 Cover the pan and take it off the heat. Let it rest for 6 minutes. Remove and pat dry the chicken tenders, then put them on serving plates with radish sprouts, to taste.

Note

The key here is to turn the heat off as soon as you put in the chicken tenders and to cook them with residual heat. The tenders can also be sliced or shredded! The cooking liquid can be seasoned with additional salt koji, if you wish, to turn it into a soup.

Salt Koji

Yogurt Potato Salad

Using yogurt for this potato salad gives it a refreshing yet rich flavor! It is recommended on hot days.

Serves 4–5

STORAGE TIME: Place in a storage container and refrigerate for 2–3 days.

⅓ cup (50 g) cucumber
A pinch of salt
⅓ cup (50 g) onion
2 slices ham
2 cups (300 g) potatoes

A ingredients
3 tablespoons plain yogurt
1 tablespoon olive oil
¼ teaspoon salt

1 Slice the cucumber thinly and place in a bowl. Sprinkle with a pinch of salt and rub it in well. Slice the onion in half horizontally then slice thinly with the grain. Place in a microwave safe container and cover loosely with cling film. Microwave for about 1 minute. Cut the ham slices in half then cut into ⅓ inch (1 cm) strips.

2 Wash the potatoes well. Wrap each wet potato without peeling them in cling film. Place in a microwave safe container and microwave for about 3 minutes 30 seconds. Take the potatoes out, turn them over and microwave for an additional 3 minutes.

3 Peel the potatoes while they are still hot, holding them with a moist kitchen towel to prevent burning yourself (**photo b**). Mash up roughly with a spoon, and leave to cool.

4 Add the A ingredients to the mashed potatoes and mix well. Add the cucumber, onion and ham and mix to combine.

Salt Koji Coleslaw

This only needs to be mixed, so it's a handy side dish that's great for bentos too!

Serves 2

STORAGE TIME: Can be refrigerated for 3 to 4 days in a storage container.

3 cups (300 g) cabbage
2 tablespoons salt koji
1 tablespoon olive oil
1 tablespoon rice vinegar

Salt Koji

1 Core the cabbage and shred the leaves, placing them in a bowl. Add the salt koji and rub it in. Let it marinate for about 10 minutes.
2 Squeeze the moisture out of the shredded cabbage. Add the olive oil and the rice vinegar and mix well.

Shredded Carrot with Amazake

A family favorite, this dish has a gentle sweetness.

Serves 2

STORAGE TIME: Refrigerate for up to 3 to 4 days in a storage

1 medium carrot (2 oz/60 g)
1 teaspoon olive oil

A ingredients:
2 tablespoons undiluted amazake
2 teaspoons soy sauce
2 teaspoons rice vinegar

Amazake

1 Peel the carrot and shred into 1½–2-inch (4–5-cm) pieces.
2 Heat the olive oil in a skillet over medium. Add the shredded carrot and stir fry. When the carrot's wilted, add the A ingredients, stir fry quickly and serve.

Chapter 5

Healthy Sweets and Snacks

If you use amazake instead of sugar, you can make healthy treats with a gentle hint of sweetness. Add the power of fermentation to your desserts and sweet snacks and give yourself a guilt-free break. These recipes are perfect as daily snacks or as treats for the kids when you want to provide them with a healthier option.

Homemade Amazake Banana Ice Cream

Everyone loves this chocolate banana ice cream with its gentle sweetness.

Serves 3–4

⅓ cup (100 ml) double concentrate amazake
⅓ cup (100 ml) unsweetened soy milk
1 banana
1 tablespoon lemon juice
Cacao nibs or chopped dark chocolate, to taste

1 Put the amazake, soy milk, banana and lemon juice in a blender and process until smooth. Put the liquid into a freezer container. Close the lid and freeze. Mix it up a couple of times every 2 hours with a spoon.
2 Leave at room temperature for about 5 minutes and mix well. Serve in bowls topped with cacao nibs or dark chocolate.

Note
If you mix up the liquid in a blender instead of with a spoon, the results will be even smoother.

Amazake

Tomato and Umeboshi Amazake Sherbert

The umeboshi flavor of this unique ice cream is addictive.

Amazake

Serves 3–4

½ cup (140 ml) double concentrate amazake
¾ cup (150 g) ripe tomatoes
3 tablespoons unsweetened soy milk
2 umeboshi

1 Core and deseed the tomatoes. Put the amazake, tomatoes and soy milk in a blender and process until smooth. Put the blended liquid in a freezer container. Pit the umeboshi, break them into pieces and add them to the liquid. Mix lightly. Cover with a lid and freeze. Mix with a spoon a couple of times every 2 hours.
2 Leave at room temperature for about 5 minutes, then mix well. Serve in bowls.

Amazake

Homemade Amazake Tofu Ice Cream

The smooth texture of the tofu and the richness of the amazake make this a creamy treat you'll add to your list of cravings.

Serves 3–4

⅔ **cup (150 g) silken tofu**
⅔ **cup (150 ml) double concentrate amazake**
1 tablespoon lemon juice
A pinch of salt
Mint leaves, to garnish

1 Wrap the tofu in a double layer of paper towels and place it in a microwave-safe dish (**photo a**). Microwave on high for about 1 minute 30 seconds, then drain off the water and let the tofu cool.
2 Put the tofu, amazake, lemon juice and salt in a blender and process until smooth. Transfer the liquid to a freezer container,

cover it with a lid and freeze. Mix the contents with a spoon a couple of times every 2 hours.
3 Leave it at room temperature for about 5 minutes, then mix well. Serve in bowls, topped with mint leaves.

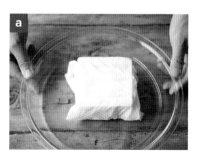

Strawberry Yogurt Parfait

Refreshingly light yogurt cream is used instead of whipped cream. The parfait can always be made with the seasonal fruit of your choice instead of strawberries.

Serves 2 in 2 small glasses

12 strawberries
4 plain vanilla cookies
Just less than 1 cup (220 g)
 strained yogurt (see page 67,
 or use Greek yogurt instead)
1 tablespoon milk
1½ tablespoons honey

1 Hull the strawberries. Reserve two to use as a topping, cutting the rest into ⅓-inch (1-cm) dice. Roughly crush the cookies. Put the yogurt, milk and honey in a bowl, and mix with a whisk to turn it into a cream.
2 Put the crushed cookies, diced strawberries and yogurt cream in layers in the parfait glasses. Top each one with a strawberry.

Yogurt

Amazake

Amazake Mochi Dumplings

By simply mixing amazake and potato starch or cornstarch together, you can easily make this classic Japanese sweet.

Serves 2–3

1 cup (220 ml) undiluted
    amazake
3 tablespoons potato starch or
    cornstarch

A ingredients:
3 tablespoons kinako (roasted
    soybean powder)
1 tablespoon sugar
A pinch of coarse salt

B ingredients:
3 tablespoons ground black
    sesame seeds
1 tablespoon sugar
A pinch of coarse salt

1 Put the A and B ingredients into their own shallow containers and mix well.
2 Put the amazake and potato or cornstarch in a pan and mix. Heat over medium-low. Cook while continuously mixing with a wooden spatula until it;s sticky. Reduce the heat to low while continuing to mix the dough.
3 When the dough is very

Note

It's important to keep mixing the dough until it's very sticky. A soft and chewy texture is what you're going for.

sticky, form it into dumplings using a wet spoon. Coat the dough with the A and B ingredients respectively.

Miso

White Miso Shortbread Cookies

Easy butter-free cookies that you just mix and bake! Make them whenever you feel like it.

Makes 28 1½-inch (3.5-cm) cookies

½ cup (75 g) cake flour
⅓ cup (25 g) almond powder
⅓ cup (25 g) sugar
2 tablespoons unroasted white sesame oil
  or vegetable oil
½ beaten egg
1 tablespoon white miso
Chopped peanuts, to top
A pinch of salt

1 Put the cake flour, almond powder, cane sugar and salt in a bowl and mix well.
2 Add the oil to the bowl and mix in with a spoon. Mix together with your hands until the dough is crumbly. Add the beaten egg and miso and mix it in with your hands. Form the dough into a ball.
3 Preheat the oven to 340°F (170°C). Sandwich the dough between sheets of plastic wrap and roll it out with a rolling pin. Cut the dough out with a cookie cutter. Line a baking sheet with parchment paper and line it with the cut-out cookies. Top the cookies with chopped peanuts. Bake in the preheated oven for 10 to 13 minutes, then cool on a rack.

Note
White miso has a sweet flavor that matches well with sweet treats like cookies. You can use salted or unsalted peanuts. If it looks like the cookies are getting too brown, cover them with aluminum foil as they bake.

Amazake French Toast

Richly flavored French toast that has soaked up the batter overnight.

Serves 2

1 egg
⅔ cup (150 ml) undiluted amazake
3 tablespoons and 2 teaspoons unsweetened soy milk
2 thick slices sliced bread
2 teaspoons butter
Maple syrup or honey, to serve

1 Put the egg in a bowl and beat it well. Add the amazake and soy milk and mix.

2 Cut the bread slices in half and place them in a plastic bag. Add the Step 1 mixture and move the bag around so that the bread absorbs the liquid evenly. Place it in a shallow container (**photo a**). Refrigerate overnight, turning the contents once.

3 Melt the butter in a skillet over low heat. Take the Step 2 bread slices out of the bag and put them into the skillet. Panfry for about 5 minutes or until browned. Turn the bread slices over, cover the pan and fry for another 5 minutes or so. Transfer the pieces to serving plates and drizzle with maple syrup or honey, to taste.

Note

By soaking the bread in a plastic bag, it will absorb the liquid thoroughly. The amazake contributes a gentle sweetness so add maple syrup or honey to taste.

Amazake

Parmesan Sake Lees Bread Sticks

Flavored with Parmesan cheese, these crackers are a great match with a glass of wine!

Serves 2–3

¼ cup (50 g) cake flour
1 tablespoon grated Parmesan cheese
A pinch of salt
1 tablespoon olive oil
⅛ cup (25 g) sake lees paste

1 Preheat the oven to 340°F (170°C). Put the cake flour, grated cheese and salt in a bowl and mix well. Add the olive oil and rub it into the dry ingredients until crumbly. Add the sake lees and 2 teaspoons of water to the dough, mixing it in with your hands. Form the dough into a ball.
2 Sandwich the dough between two sheets of plastic wrap and roll it out into a 4-inch by 10-inch (10-cm by 26-cm) rectangle. Cut into ⅓-inch-wide (1-cm) x 4-inch-ling (10-cm) sticks.
3 Line a baking sheet with parchment paper. Line the sheet with the pieces of dough and poke holes in them with a fork. Bake in the preheated oven for 10 to 15 minutes, then transfer to a rack to cool.

Note

If you're using sheet sake lees (see page 19), put ⅛ cup (25 g) into a small microwave-safe container, add 1 teaspoon water and cover loosely with plastic wrap. Microwave for about 20 seconds and mix well before using. If you poke the dough with a fork, air will escape from the holes so that the crackers will bake evenly. If it looks like the crackers are browning too quickly, top them with aluminum foil.

Sake lees

Amazake

Amazake Sweet Red Bean Dessert

An easy oshiruko that's made by simply mixing anko (or adzuki bean paste) with amazake.

Serves 2

⅔ cup (220 g) canned or vacuum-packed anko (sweet adzuki bean paste)

A little more than ⅓ cup (100 ml) undiluted amazake

2 square mochi pieces, to garnish

1 Put the anko and amazake in a pan over medium-low heat, and heat up while diluting the anko.

2 Cut the mochi squares in half, and grill in a toaster oven or on a grill. Distribute the Step 1 mix equally in serving bowls, and top with 2 pieces each of the mochi.

 Note

Taste it, and if it needs more sweetness, then add a little sugar!

Sake Lees Cheesecake

The sake lees create a hidden flavor in this cheesecake adding richness and a deep, pleasing fragrance.

Makes one 6-inch (15-cm) round cake

¼ cup (50 g) sake lees paste
1 cup (210 g) cream cheese, at room temperature
¼ cup (50 g) granulated sugar or caster sugar
⅓ cup (80 ml) heavy cream
1 beaten egg, at room temperature
2 tablespoons cake flour

1 Preheat the oven to 350°F (180°C). Put the sake lees and cream cheese in a large bowl, then mix with a rubber spatula until smooth (**photo a**). Add the sugar and mix until smooth.

2 Add the heavy cream a little bit at a time, whisking quickly after each addition (**photo b**). When the mixture is smooth, sift in the cake flour and cut it into the batter.

3 When the batter is combined, pour it in the cake tin and smooth the surface. Lift then gently drop it onto your countertop several times to get rid of any air bubbles (**photo c**).

4 Place the cake tin on a baking sheet and bake in the preheated oven for 40 to 50 minutes or until a wooden skewer inserted in the middle comes out clean. Let cool in the cake tin (**photo d**), then refrigerate overnight. Cut into slices and serve.

 Note

If you're using sheet sake lees (see page 19), put ¼ cup (50 g) into a small microwave-safe container, add 1 tablespoon water and cover loosely with plastic wrap. Microwave for about 30 seconds and mix well before using. Don't overmix the batter after adding the cake flour. Just gently fold it in. If you turn the cake tin halfway through baking, it will brown nicely. The baked cheesecake can be cut into individually wrapped slices and frozen for about a month. Just defrost the pieces in the refrigerator and enjoy.

Final Fermentation Thoughts

Our journey has come to an end, but I hope you make it a daily one, as a friend of fermentation, integrating the wholesome goodness and fabulous flavor of these foods into every meal.

Fermentation for life: it's more than just a tagline but a healthful habit and a daily practice that enriches as it energizes.

I've shared with you here my personal hits, easy recipes that I make on an ongoing if not daily basis. The focus really is on ease, simple substitutions and easy integrations you can make whether you're busy with work or home life. It just takes a few minutes to unlock these savory and sweet secrets.

I'd like to take this opportunity to thank everyone involved in the creation of the original edition of this book. The editorial staff at Orange Page, including Ms. Akiyama and Ms. Hira, proved invaluable. And the head designer, Ms. Nomoto, is the reason this book is so clearly laid out, easy to understand and of course incredibly appealing!

I'd also like to thank my husband, who was in charge of the photography and also helped me with the cooking.

Above all, I couldn't do this without the help and support of all of you who have picked up this book and continue to cheer me on. I thank you all from the bottom of my heart. I hope I've made even more fermentation friends along the way!

—Misa Enomoto

Fermented Recipe Index

Here's a list of the recipes in this book organized by the fermented food that's used. Use this index when you think, "I want to eat some miso today" or "I've got a sudden craving for amazake." (Note: Of the recipes that use more than two fermented foods, only the ones that use miso + mirin + black vinegar are included here.)

Published by Tuttle Publishing, an imprint of
Periplus Editions (HK) Ltd.

www.tuttlepublishing.com

YURU HAKKO MISO, AMAZAKE, NATTO, YOGURT.
IMASUGU HAJIMERARERU, MAINICHI TSUZU-
KERARERU
© 2022 Misa Enomoto
English translation rights arranged with
The Orangepage Inc. through Japan UNI Agency, Inc.,
Tokyo

English Translation © 2024 by Periplus Editions
(HK) Ltd.

Library of Congress Cataloging-in-Publication
Data in process

ISBN 978-4-8053-1806-5

27 26 25 24   10 9 8 7 6 5 4 3 2 1
Printed in China   2407EP

Distributed by

North America, Latin America & Europe
Tuttle Publishing
364 Innovation Drive
North Clarendon, VT 05759-9436 U.S.A.
Tel: 1 (802) 773 8930
Fax: 1 (802) 773 6993
info@tuttlepublishing.com
www.tuttlepublishing.com

Japan
Tuttle Publishing
Yaekari Building, 3rd Floor
5-4-12 Osaki
Shinagawa-ku
Tokyo 141 0032
Tel: (81) 3 5437 0171
Fax: (81) 3 5437 0755
sales@tuttle.co.jp
www.tuttle.co.jp

Asia Pacific
Berkeley Books Pte. Ltd.
3 Kallang Sector, #04-01
Singapore 349278
Tel: (65) 6741 2178
Fax: (65) 6741 2179
inquiries@periplus.com.sg
www.tuttlepublishing.com

"Books to Span the East and West"

Tuttle Publishing was founded in 1832 in the small New England town of Rutland, Vermont [USA].
Our core values remain as strong today as they were then—to publish best-in-class books which bring
people together one page at a time. In 1948, we established a publishing outpost in Japan—and Tuttle
is now a leader in publishing English-language books about the arts, languages and cultures of Asia.
The world has become a much smaller place today and Asia's economic and cultural influence has
grown. Yet the need for meaningful dialogue and information about this diverse region has never been
greater. Over the past seven decades, Tuttle has published thousands of books on subjects ranging
from martial arts and paper crafts to language learning and literature—and our talented authors,
illustrators, designers and photographers have won many prestigious awards. We welcome you to
explore the wealth of information available on Asia at **www.tuttlepublishing.com**.